980

FRANCISCO PIZARRO

(From an Original Painting in the Palace of the Viceroys at Lima, Peru)

Makers of South America

BY
MARGARETTE DANIELS

THE METHODIST BOOK CONCERN
NEW YORK   CINCINNATI

CONTENTS

ILLUSTRATIONS

PREFACE

Some day we are going to know our friends in the other America a great deal better than we do now. Big ships are plying back and forth through the new canal, and every year it grows a little easier to travel in South America. Nowadays a trip to Callao is likely to be advertised by enterprising steamship companies along with tours to Bermuda or over the Great Lakes.

Here are twelve men who have done big things for those countries beyond Panama—the men who ought to head our list of South American acquaintances. Whether a patriot like San Martin, or a rascal like Pizarro; loved by his countrymen like Bolivar, or hated like Rosas; a brilliant success like Mr. Grubb, or a failure like Allen Gardiner—all had their share in the making of the continent, as Washington and Jackson and Lincoln helped in the making of our country.

Lord James Bryce, the Englishman who has written the best history of the United States, went down to South America not long ago, prowled around for a few months, and then wrote the finest volume of general information about the whole country that we have ever had. In *South America: Observations and Impressions,* he has selected just the things about each republic, past and present, that every one wants

to know—history, romance, people and places, anecdotes, adventures and legends. William Prescott's
Conquest of Peru, the story of the glorious Inca
dynasty and old Pizarro's hairbreadth escapes, we have
most of us read long before this in the days when we
pored over *Ivanhoe* and *The Last of the Mohicans.*
For the story of the picturesque old mission towns of
Argentine and Paraguay, the Arcadia where the Jesuit
fathers once collected the Guarani Indians, there is
W. H. Koebel's *In Jesuit Land.* The best book on the
wars for independence will not be so easy to find in
your library, but it is worth hunting for. It is called
The Emancipation of South America, and Bartolomé
Mitre, one of the greatest historians of his country,
wrote it. The translator has left out some cumber-
some details, but if it still seems overdetailed for general reading, it is easy to skip without missing the
main points and the thrilling accounts of men and
battles. You will find in it many anecdotes of San
Martin and Bolivar, the battles they fought, the men
who helped them, and the story of their mysterious
interview. In those days it seems to have been the
fashion for every sea captain and army officer to
keep a journal and find some one to publish it for
him. Captain Basil Hall's *Journal of Travels in
Chile and Peru* is the best of dozens you might read.
He was cruising along the western coast just at the
time that San Martin went to Lima, and he tells story
after story of what happened during the campaign, of
meeting the great general, of picnics and balls and

merrymaking, and the customs of the people. *An Unknown People in an Unknown Land,* written by Mr. Grubb, is packed full of his adventures in the Chaco, a region where few white men have ever dared to go, and tells how he made friends of the Indians who used to depend on the skulls of intruders for their supply of drinking cups. For a general history of the continent, from the time of the old navigators who discovered the coast of America when they were looking for India and the Spice Islands, down to the present, read *South American Republics,* by Thomas Dawson. The account of each country is given separately.

Thanks are due to the American Bible Society and to the Presbyterian Board of Foreign Missions for the use of annual reports and correspondence; to the librarian of Fordham University for permission to read a rare book on the life of Padre Anchieta; and to Mr. E. E. Olcott for information which has not been published before, given me in an entertaining interview at his office down on the New York waterfront.

M. D.

Lower Warner, New Hampshire
August 1, 1916

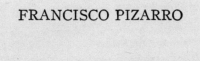

FRANCISCO PIZARRO

FRANCISCO PIZARRO

On a large farm in Truxillo, a town of old Spain, about the time that Columbus discovered America, young Francisco Pizarro held the useful but unromantic position of swineherd. His parents cared nothing for him, he hardly knew what a piece of money looked like, no one ever thought of teaching him to read or write; but his heart was full of pluck, and his head of vague plans for great adventures. Those were exciting years in Spain, for wonderful stories of her new possessions poured across the Atlantic, and certainly lost nothing in glamour and romance as they were repeated. Sailing off to an unknown land on an uncharted sea held no terrors for Pizarro, and the rumors of gold-mines sounded pleasantly in his ears. Fired with ambition to begin life afresh, in 1509 he set out from Seville for the New World where all men stood an equal chance of winning fame and treasure. His baggage consisted of a sword and a cloak. His two sole assets were pure grit, and a dogged perseverance that knocked difficulties out of the way like ninepins.

As yet only a small fragment of America had been explored: the West Indies where Columbus landed on his first voyage; the Atlantic coast region of

3

what is now Central America; and the neighboring South American shore to the east of the Isthmus of Panama, or Darien as it was called then. By the end of ten years Pizarro was neither rich nor famous, but he had made a name and place for himself in the new colony, and was engaged in raising cattle with a business partner named Almagro. He owned his own house on the outskirts of the city of Panama, his farm and his Indian servants, and was held "as one of the principal people in the land . . . having distinguished himself in the conquest and settling, and in the services of his Majesty." During these years Pizarro had many times experienced the emergencies and hardships of the explorer's life, and he had seen before his eyes the rainbow vision of gold. A hard worker, afraid of nothing under the sun, always dependable, he became the right-hand man of Balboa, who was a leading spirit in many excursions over the isthmus.

Balboa, unlike most of these Spanish leaders, was diplomatic in his relations with the Indians, and soon made friends with the caciques, or chiefs, of neighboring tribes. It was in 1511, when they were paying a visit in the home of a powerful cacique named Comogre, that Pizarro and Balboa first heard the dazzling tale of the wealth of Peru. As a polite little attention their host presented them with many golden trinkets. At this windfall the guests completely lost their heads and good manners and began such a "brabbling" about the dividing of the gold, that the dignified Indians listened in astonishment and disgust.

Finally, as the chief's son stood watching the beautiful ornaments being weighed and haggled over as if each Spaniard's life depended on grabbing the most, he lost his temper and struck the scales with his fist. As the gold scattered about the room he cried the fateful words which led to the conquest of Peru:

"What is this, Christians; is it for such a little thing that you quarrel? If this is what you prize so much that you are willing to leave your distant homes and to risk life itself, I can tell you of a land where they eat and drink out of golden vessels, and gold is as cheap as iron is with you." The Indian prince pointed toward the west, and told about a sea of which the white men had never heard. It lay beyond the mountains of the isthmus, and whoever would find the land of gold must sail south for a distance of six suns. "But," he added, "it is necessary for this that you should be more in number than you are now, for you would have to fight your way with great kings."

Two years later Balboa proved the truth of the Indian's words when he crossed the isthmus and discovered the Pacific Ocean. Pizarro, his chief lieutenant, was the first man to scramble after him to the top of a high peak and look down upon the southern sea. When this news reached the court of Spain the king appointed a governor named Pedrarias to go to the isthmus and superintend the sending out of expeditions to the south. Hundreds of adventurers clamored to sail with him, for they had heard that in the

New World "the sands sparkled with gems, and golden pebbles as large as birds' eggs were dragged in nets out of the rivers."

The 1,500 men who set out for Panama with such high hopes found disease and fever instead of gems, and hunger instead of gold. In the first month 700 died. The cavaliers in their brocaded court costumes could be seen in the streets choking down grass to keep themselves alive, or trying to exchange a gorgeous embroidered cloak for a pound of Indian meal. As time went on a few adventurers who had sailed a little way down the coast brought back gloomy reports, and most of the colonists had had enough of expeditions which usually turned out to be all danger and no reward. Pizarro saw his opportunity. He was over fifty years old then, but he had lost none of his adventurous spirit, and if there was any gold in Peru he determined to find it.

In 1524 he and his partner sold their farm, and with a third associate formed a company to fit out an expedition. Each promised to contribute his entire fortune, and since Pizarro had the least money he agreed to do the most dangerous part of the work, the taking command of the exploring party. It was almost impossible to find volunteers, and the crew had to be made up largely of newcomers who had no idea what lay in store for them, and "black sheep" who felt that they could be no worse off than they already were.

By the end of the year one little ship was tossing its

way through heavy tempests along the shores of an unknown land, and one hundred miserable men were complaining bitterly because Pizarro had brought them on a wild-goose chase. They had found neither food nor inhabitants, only tangled, dripping forests and vast swamps. Sheets of rain closed in about them day and night; they could see nothing but the black, angry ocean and gray sky; none knew where they were going or what worse horrors lay in store for them. The ship had to be sent back for supplies and while it was gone twenty-seven of the men who remained behind with Pizarro died of exposure and starvation. When they finally discovered a few solitary hamlets, the Indians were suspicious and unfriendly and attacked the little party. Only Pizarro's fierce bravery, so spectacular that it awed the Indians, saved the expedition from ending then and there. No explorers ever chose a worse time of year or wore a more inappropriate costume; there in the dreadful humidity of the rainy season, right in the region of the equator, these poor soldiers, every time they landed to search for food or villages, had to drag along as best they could under the weight of full suits of armor.

It was all a dismal failure, but Pizarro had not the slightest intention of going back empty-handed. Instead he went back part of the way and waited until another expedition could be organized by his partners. Then he started out all over again. For 500 miles he sailed along the coast of what is now Colombia, and the farther his ship went the more mythical seemed the great empire he was seeking. Again and again the ship would have to be sent back for supplies or repairs, while Pizarro and some of his men stayed behind in the midst of every danger of disease, starvation and Indians. Through all these periods of desolate waiting Pizarro never allowed himself to show a moment's discouragement before his soldiers. No one worked harder than he in foraging for food, and in caring for those who were too weak to look out for themselves. "In labors and dangers he was ever the first." Whenever he had a chance he would remind the men of the great rewards that lay before them, the gold they were going to find, and the triumph of bringing it home to show the scoffers in Panama.

When the ship returned they would sail a little farther. One time when Pizarro landed, hoping to have a chat with the Indians, an ominous troop of warriors gathered on the beach. The only thing that saved the Spaniards, too few in number to protect themselves, was a cavalier who fell off his horse. The Indians had never seen a horse before, and supposed that horse and rider were all one great monster. When they saw it divide into two pieces they fell back in alarm and the Spaniards had time to hurry on board their ship.

The greatest difficulty always came when Almagro would go back for supplies. On one occasion the soldiers, angry at the thought of another long, miserable wait, wrote letters to their friends protesting against "the cold-blooded manner in which they were to be sacrificed to the obstinate cupidity of their leaders." These letters Pizarro ordered to be destroyed, but one ingenious soul wrote a gloomy account of all their sufferings and hid it in a ball of wool which he sent to the governor's wife as a sample of a product of the country. He added a postscript in the form of a rhyme which caused great excitement in Panama:

> "Look out, Señor Governor,
> For the drover while he's near;
> Since he goes home to get the sheep
> For the butcher who stays here."

This not only prevented any new volunteers from joining the expedition, but the governor was so enraged at the loss of life and at Pizarro's stubbornness that he sent off two ships with orders for every Spaniard to return. When the ships came to take them back to home and comfort, Pizarro and his men were half dead with hunger and exposure, and so haggard and unkempt that they were hardly recognizable.

Pizarro had sunk his whole fortune in this enterprise. His good name depended on it. He was not a young man with the world before him. Life would hold nothing more if this great hazard failed. It was an investment and he intended to collect the dividends. With the ships riding at anchor behind him, he stood on the beach and faced his little company. Drawing his sword he traced a line in the sand from east to west. "Friends and comrades," he said, pointing with his sword as he spoke, "on that side are toil, hunger, fatigue, the drenching storm, desertion and death; on this side ease and pleasure. There lies Peru with its riches; here, Panama and its poverty. Choose, each man, what best becomes a brave Castilian. For my part I go to the south." And he stepped across the line. Thirteen others followed him and together they stood and watched the ships, bearing their companions, vanish on the horizon. They had no food, no shelter, only the clothes they wore, no ship to take them farther, and they knew nothing of the empire they were seeking. Building a crude raft, they conveyed themselves to an island not far off where they were able to shoot game with their crossbows, and there for seven months they waited for help to come.

Meanwhile the two partners in Panama argued with the stubborn old governor until they won his consent to fit out a relief ship on condition that within six months Pizarro return and report what he had been able to accomplish. It was on this little ship that Pizarro reached Peru and the Empire of the Incas.

Just three years after he had sailed from Panama, Pizarro anchored off Tumbez, on the Gulf of Guayaquil, about where Ecuador joins Peru to-day, and sent friendly messages and presents to the Indians. The messenger returned with such marvelous stories of wealth that none believed him until they had seen for themselves. There were houses of stone, vessels of gold and silver, a temple lined with plates of gold, and gardens adorned with animals carved from gold. The

Spaniards went wild with joy; the last grumbling
skeptic had to admit that they had found their El
Dorado. The Indians were generous and hospitable,
and when the six months were nearly over Pizarro had
been presented with enough gold ornaments and llamas
to convince any one of the glorious success of his expedition, and he returned to Panama in triumph. But
a new governor now held sway on the isthmus, and he
refused to be impressed with Pizarro's report. "I
have no desire to build up other states at the expense
of my own," he told them; "nor throw away more lives
than have already been sacrificed by the cheap display
of gold and silver toys and a few Indian sheep." The
three partners had no more money. Yet there lay the
magic empire waiting to be plundered, the greatest
prize a nation ever dreamed of appropriating. Pizarro
made up his mind to go to Spain and tell his wonderful
story to the king, Charles V, carrying with him specimens of the treasures he had found. Charles,
impressed with the sincerity and reliability of the rough
old soldier, appointed him governor of Peru with the
title of marquis, and put into his capable hands the
double duty of converting the Indians and stealing
their empire.

This race of Indians, whose country stretched for
2,000 miles along the western coast, were far more
intelligent and civilized than any other natives of the
western hemisphere with the exception of the Aztecs
of Mexico. Their government was orderly and prosperous, a veritable Utopia founded upon implicit obe-

dience to their king, called the Inca, and devoted worship of their deity, the sun-god. Land and work were allotted to the head of each family, and rigid laws protected the lives and rights of the people. Not a foot of land was wasted. By a remarkable system of irrigation dry ground was prepared for cultivation; the Indians had spent years of labor in making land by carrying earth in baskets and covering up the bare rocks. Their fine roads and fortresses, and the plentiful provisions of grain which they thriftily stored away in their great granaries each year were used to good purpose by the Spaniards and in no small degree helped them in the conquest.

Within two years the conquerors, or *conquistadores,* though at no time numbering more than 300, had subdued these hordes of prosperous, contented Indians, and had replaced the Inca dynasty with the first Spanish viceroyalty. The real stimulus behind all their bravery and sacrifice was wealth and fame; religion was their ostensible reason for the conquest, and in the name of the Church they practised all the cruelties and treacheries necessary to crush the empire.

When Pizarro arrived in Peru an Inca had just died and bequeathed his kingdom to two sons who were now fighting each other. In the midst of the war Atahualpa, Inca of the northern half, heard that a party of strange white men had landed in his country, that they carried extraordinary weapons, and rode upon great, terrifying beasts which galloped over the ground with marvelous speed. He consented to an interview with the white chief. With a force of about 150 soldiers the dauntless Pizarro struck into the heart of the Indian territory. In the native city of Cajamarca, 200 miles south of San Miguel, the first Spanish settlement, he met the Inca.

Pizarro had conceived a plan so daring that another man would never have dreamed of its possibility. He believed there was only one way for so small a band of men to conquer so great a nation. Atahualpa must be kidnapped. The Indians from the beginning of their national existence had been so completely under the domination of their Inca, whom they believed to be a divine being, that without him they must fall into utter confusion. If, as Pizarro reasoned, the Inca with his huge armies had treacherous designs on the Spaniards, their only hope lay in trapping Atahualpa before he could trap them. In the open square in the middle of the city he pitched his camp and sent word to the Inca that he was waiting to receive him as "a friend and a brother."

The next morning the royal procession passed through the city gates. First came 300 Indian boys with bows and arrows, singing, followed by 1,000 men resplendent in livery of red and white squares like a chess-board. Other troops wore pure white and carried silver hammers. Eighty chiefs in costumes of azure blue bore the glittering throne of the Inca in an open litter high above their heads. As Atahualpa approached the square not a Spanish soldier was in sight, but a priest, Pizarro's chaplain, stepped forward to greet him, with a Bible in one hand and a crucifix in the other. The pope, he announced briskly, had commissioned the greatest monarch on earth to conquer and convert this land and people, and in a learned theological discourse he pointed out to the Indians the necessity of being baptized at once. The Inca gravely inquired where he had learned these things.

"In this," said the priest, handing him the Bible.

The Inca opened the book eagerly and held it up to his ear.

"This is silent," he said. "It tells me nothing," and he threw it to the ground.

This so enraged the priest that he cried to the Spaniards: "To arms, Christians, to arms! Set on at once! I absolve you."

The governor gave the signal and the soldiers rushed from their hiding-places. With their horses, muskets and swords, they terrified and slaughtered the helpless Indians until they fled in confusion. Pizarro himself snatched the Inca from his throne and carried him off to the Spanish camp.

The governor treated the prisoner with much kindness. The Indian was quick and intelligent. In twenty days he had learned enough Spanish to converse with his jailers, and was a good match for them in chess and cards. He soon perceived that what the Spaniards were after was gold. One day he made a bargain with Pizarro. In return for his freedom he promised to fill the whole room in which they were standing as high as he could reach with gold ornaments. The room was seventeen feet wide and twenty-two feet long, and the point he had touched on the wall was nine feet from the floor. He dispatched his messengers to all parts of the empire, and the Spaniards marveled at the treasure which was being heaped up in their camp without effort on their part. As the gold in the room rose higher and higher they became too impatient to wait until all of it had been brought; they began the melting and weighing. When all was ready for division the entire amount was valued at the equivalent of $15,500,000, the largest sum in gold that men ever saw in one place at one time. One fifth had to be reserved for the crown; the rest was divided among the men. The outcome of the adventure was far greater than the wildest hopes and dreams of those who shared in it.

Now that Atahualpa had paid his magnificent ransom he naturally demanded his freedom. But Pizarro knew too well the danger of allowing the Inca to return to his own people. On the pretext of punishment for conspiracy, of which there was never one particle of evidence, he was condemned to death after the formality of a mock trial.

"What have I or my children done, that I should meet such a fate? From your hands too," he said to Pizarro; "you, who have met with friendship and kindness from my people, with whom I have shared my treasures, who have received nothing but benefits from me!"

Pizarro was not the man to allow any feelings of

sympathy to stand in the way of his great enterprise. Atahualpa, the last of the Inca dynasty, was strangled in the public square. There were many fierce battles with the Indians after that time, but they never recovered their power. They had always been dominated by any force which they believed mightier than themselves—their Inca, the sun-god, and now the Spaniards. They never really believed they were capable of resisting the white men whom they thought so vastly superior to themselves; and this racial lack of self-confidence was the reason for their downfall.

Associated with Pizarro in the conquest were his three brothers, all as valiant and persevering as himself. While they took command of the Spanish troops, the governor with his extraordinary executive ability began to plan for settlements and cities. In a fine strategical position, near the coast and connected with the Indian cities by the Inca's military roads, Pizarro founded Lima. All the Indians living within a hundred-mile radius were mustered to lay out streets and build houses. Farther up the coast Truxillo, named after the governor's birthplace, was founded as headquarters for the northern region.

The soldiers explored in all directions, plundering palaces and temples in their search for gold. In Cuzco, capital of the empire, they found a mine of wealth in every building, and in a cavern near the city, where the Indians had tried to conceal them, they found ten statues of women and four of llamas wrought from gold and silver. "Merely to see them," writes one of the Spaniards naïvely, "was truly a great satisfaction."

As soon as the Indians found what the Spaniards were hunting for, they began to hide their treasures. All the gold which Atahualpa collected is said to be far less than the amount which the Indians buried or threw into lakes because they could no longer guard it. Many years later an Indian once took a large measure of maize, and dropping one grain out of it, said to the white men: "The Christians have found just so much; the rest is so concealed that we ourselves do not know the place of it."

The rough soldiers, most of whom had never known what it meant to have money to spend, now became habitual gamblers, and many a night with one throw of the dice or flip of a card a man would lose all the treasure he had sacrificed so much to win.

As the news of the conquest reached Europe other adventurers flocked to Peru. One of them wrote: "I determined to go to Peru, a newly discovered land, where there is an infinite quantity of gold. But the gold is not to be obtained for nothing, for 80 men out of every 100 who go in search of it die. It is very certain that a great prize is never gained at small cost." Another cavalier told his friends: "I declare, on my faith that, if they offered to make me a king on condition that I went through all this again, I would not do it, but I would rather be a doctor's stirrup boy."

While Pizarro was building his city of Lima, he heard that Cuzco had been burned to the ground by the Indians, and that his brothers were holding the fortress against the besiegers. Before he could send them aid worse news reached him. Almagro, who had been granted by royal permit the privilege of conquering and plundering the southern half of the empire, where Chile is to-day, had returned from a fruitless journey. The tribes in the south, which had been subdued previously by the Incas, were poor and ignorant, and Almagro was dissatisfied with his share of the bargain. Finding Pizarro's men in Cuzco worn out after their months of fighting, he attacked them and took the city himself. Civil war now supplanted Indian wars. The two Spanish factions engaged in a fiercer battle than the natives had ever seen, and from the surrounding heights the Indian spectators yelled in triumph as they watched their enemies kill each other. Almagro was captured and executed by the orders of one of the brothers, Hernando Pizarro, the governor refusing to intercede to save the life of his old friend and business partner.

The followers of Almagro, called "Men of Chile," who had shared their leader's ambitions, were bitter enemies of Pizarro and stirred up much discontent in Lima. The governor was constantly warned of his personal danger from conspiracies and urged to banish the offenders from the colony, but he hardly gave the matter a second thought. "Be in no pain," he told his friends, "about my life; it is perfectly safe as long as every man in Peru knows that I can in a moment cut off any head which dares to harbor a thought against me."

One day in June, 1541, while Pizarro was dining with twenty guests in his own house, a band of "Men of Chile" broke into the entrance hall. "To arms! The Men of Chile are coming to kill the marquis!" cried a page. Most of the guests dropped through the open windows into the garden below. Pizarro rushed forward to meet the assassins as they poured into the dining-room. "What shameful thing is this?" he cried. "Why do you wish to kill me?" He was over seventy years old, but he fought so valiantly that the struggle lasted several minutes, and two of the conspirators were killed. Then some one exclaimed: "Why are we so long about it? Down with the tyrant!" and they dashed his brains out upon the stone floor. "The old lion died fighting and, in his death agonies, kissed the sign of the cross, which he traced on the floor, in blood which flowed from his own veins."

The Men of Chile poured into the streets at the news of the governor's death and took possession of the city.

A viceroy was sent out by the king to rule in Pizarro's place, and as settlers began to flock to the new country, Spanish colonies grew up like magic. The invaders became a ruling caste dependent for their livelihood on the unpaid labor of their Indian serfs, who worked the mines and tilled the land which had once been their own. The race, but a few years back so contented and prosperous, became a race of slaves, almost without exception treated harshly or cruelly by their masters. The atrocities of Spanish officials two and three hundred years later, James Bryce says, "were at once the evidence of what Spanish rule in Peru had been and a prestige of its fall. . . . There were dark sides to the ancient civilization, but was it worth destroying in order to erect on its ruins what the Conquerors brought to Peru?"

JOSÉ DE ANCHIETA

JOSÉ DE ANCHIETA

JOSÉ DE ANCHIETA

In the midst of the ancient forests of Misiones, a province in northern Argentina, half hidden by banks of gorgeous wildflowers and riots of shrub and fern, are a few remnants of dark stone wall, and bits of broken, moss-covered statue—all that is left of the busy Jesuit mission towns which once stretched from the coast of Brazil inland to the Paraguay and Parana Rivers. To this remote region of the world the Jesuit priests had first penetrated in the sixteenth century, and collected the wild, roving Tupi-Guarani Indians into peaceful villages with such ease and dispatch that "every one published that the new order, whose founder was born at the time Christopher Columbus began to discover the new world, had received from heaven a special mission."

The Franciscan monks who came to South America with the *conquistadores* had forced their religion upon the Indians. A few had even dared to say a good word for the poor natives, and a Dominican bishop named Las Casas had fiercely championed their cause in Mexico and Peru; but the first concentrated effort to make the Indians contented and industrious, as they had been before ever the white man appeared, and to protect them from the cruel exploitation of Portuguese and Spanish settlers, was this great enterprise of the Jesuit fathers, the earliest missionaries on the continent.

First they came to the Brazilian coast. Brazil was not Spanish territory like all the rest of the New World. A Portuguese nobleman named Cabral had happened upon the eastern shores of South America while he was trying to find the East Indies. A year later Amerigo Vespucci hurried across from Lisbon to inspect this new piece of Portuguese property, and he called the country Brazil, because, instead of the gold and silver he wanted, he found nothing of commercial value except brazil-wood, used in Europe for dyes. One of the earliest large settlements in Brazil was built up on the capacious Bay of Bahia, and when, in 1549, several hundred colonists came to live there, among them were a number of Jesuits, sent by John III of Portugal to convert the Indians, just as the Franciscans had been sent with the Spaniards by Charles V.

The priests were assigned plots of land and with their own hands chopped trees, sawed wood, hauled stones, and built a church, a college, and small houses for themselves. By that time their clothes hung in rags, they had no money, and often they were reduced to begging alms. But they had no desire for property, or comforts, or even the necessities of life. By law of their order, self-denial and the "acquisition of eternal goods" were the sole aims of a Jesuit. One father describes their early settlements: "What houses

are these that the clergy inhabit? A few miserable
straw huts. What furniture do they possess? The
breviary and manual to baptize and administer the
sacraments. What is their nourishment? Mandioca
root, beans and vegetables; and the majesty of God
is witness that they have passed twenty-four hours
without even partaking of roots, in order not to beg
of the Indians and thus become a burden to them."

When a new governor was sent to Bahia, he brought
with him more Jesuits, who scattered among the Indians in all directions, building rude settlements,
gathering the tribes together, and teaching them not
only good morals but how to work their farms.
Among these pioneers was a pale, ascetic youngster,
José de Anchieta. He had been born in Teneriffe, one
of the Canary Islands, of rich and aristocratic parents.
They sent him at fourteen to the Portuguese university
at Coimbra, where he won many honors, especially in
rhetoric, poetry and philosophy. His reputation for
brilliancy reached the ears of the Jesuits who were
always anxious to discover talented young protégés,
and by the time he was seventeen they had persuaded
him to join their order and begin training for the
priesthood. During his novitiate, part of his day's
schedule was to attend mass eight times, and his duties
at each service required such constant kneeling that
sometimes he would almost faint from exhaustion
before night. His knees grew lamer and lamer, yet
he refused to give in to what he considered a wicked
bodily weakness, and he kept his suffering secret until

he became dangerously ill. As a result of this neglect his spine was permanently injured, and all the money his father possessed could never smooth out the hump in his back. The fear that he might have to give up his training tortured him more than all the pain of his three years of illness, until he was reassured by one of the priests who predicted: "Do not worry so about it, my boy, for God intends that you shall yet serve him in this order."

Then in 1553, when the expedition was preparing to sail from Lisbon for Bahia, Anchieta's friends decided to send him along for his health. No one knew much about Brazil, but glowing reports had convinced the Portuguese that the climate and food were a sure cure for all ailments.

Anchieta reached Brazil eager to begin immediately on some branch of the mission work, and the provincial, or chief Jesuit, appointed him to go to the colony of São Paulo to start a little college for the training of young settlers who wished to join the order. There in the wilderness this teacher, twenty-one years old, gathered his pupils into the first classical school in America, instructing them in Latin, Spanish, and the Tupi language. Within a year, besides opening the school and teaching his classes, he had found time to learn the Indians' language, and to write a Tupi grammar for the use of the Jesuit missionaries.

In the report which he sent back to the provincial, he said: "Here we are, sometimes more than twenty of us together in a little hut of mud and wicker, roofed

with straw, fourteen paces long and ten wide. This is
at once the school, the infirmary, the dormitory, refec-
tory, kitchen and storehouse. Yet we covet not the
more spacious dwellings which our brethren have in
other parts. Our Lord Jesus Christ was in a far
straiter place when it was his pleasure to be born
among beasts in a manger."

The little house had no such luxury as a chimney,
and was usually so full of smoke that the classes would
adjourn to the front yard to recite under the shade
trees. A mat, hung at the entrance, served the purpose
of a door, and the pupils slept in hammocks slung from
the rafters. Banana leaves were the only dishes.

"I serve here as barber and physician," Anchieta
wrote, "physicking and bleeding the Indians, and some
of them have recovered under my hands when their
lives were despaired of." He also learned to make
alpargatas, a variety of tough shoe which could stand
hard wear. "I am now a good workman at this," he
said, "and have made many for the brethren, for it
is not possible to travel with leathern shoes among
these wilds."

There were no textbooks in this little school. The
only way of assigning lessons was for Anchieta to
write out on separate leaves copies enough to go
around. This sometimes took him all night, and the
class, when it arrived in the morning, would find its
teacher just where he had been the night before, the
pen still in his fingers. For Anchieta persistently
ignored every feeling of weariness, and forced himself

to go without sleep until he grew accustomed to the loss of it. For many hours in the night he would be on his knees in some quiet, remote spot under the stars, praying for strength to do all he saw needed to be done.

After the Tupi grammar was finished, he commenced on a dictionary. Both of these were sent to Portugal and printed there for the use of Jesuits who were preparing to work among the Indians in South America. Anchieta was not only the first scholar and the first educator, but the first poet in Brazil and the father of Brazilian literature. Instead of forbidding the Indians and the townspeople to sing their merry, ribald ballads, he wrote beautiful canticles for them which became so popular that the boys whistled them on the street, and they entirely took the place of the old songs. Some of his hymns, chanted daily by his pupils, told whole Bible stories which he had turned into verse.

Then he wrote a play, and the settlers came from far and wide to the first theatricals ever given in the New World. Like the old English morality plays, Anchieta's comedy was presented for the purpose of teaching the people a lesson, and he chose it as the most vivid way of driving home a few good morals. It was given out-of-doors on a summer afternoon. The acts of the play were written in Portuguese, but interludes in Tupi were inserted between acts so that the Indians in the audience could follow the action.

The Jesuit priests were always supposed by the

simple, ignorant people to be capable of performing wonderful miracles. Legends of the supernatural powers which Anchieta possessed would fill large volumes. All the traditional wonder-stories seem to have collected about his name. At this outdoor play he first won his reputation. After the people were all seated and the actors were about to sally forth, heavy clouds gathered, and the audience was on the verge of rushing for shelter when Anchieta appeared on the stage and held up his hand for quiet. There would be no rain, he said, until the play was over. For three hours the storm held off, and then, just as the last person reached shelter, the clouds broke and the rain poured down.

Anchieta really loved the natives and they knew it. He never regarded either an Indian or a half-breed as an inferior being. They were all his friends. Men held him in such reverence that they believed the elements and all living things obeyed his will. "The birds of the air," it was said, "formed a canopy over his head to shade him from the sun. The fish came into his net when he required them. The wild beasts of the forests attended upon him in his journeys, and served him as an escort. The winds and waves obeyed his voice. The fire, at his pleasure, undid the mischief it had done, so that bread which had been burnt to a coal in the oven was drawn out white and soft by his interference."

Reports of his remarkable powers and his influence over the wild Indians reached the ears of the provincial, and he was recalled from São Paulo for promotion.   Though not yet a priest, he was sent out on journeys into the wilderness with the Jesuit fathers who went to convert and collect into villages the roving bands of Indians.   One of his feats which won the admiration of his order was the conversion of an old Indian reprobate, aged one hundred years, who had lived long enough, one might suppose, to become set in his ways.

In small groups, often only two men together, the Jesuits pushed their way through regions where white men had never gone, exploring, learning native customs, establishing settlements.   Those who traveled with Anchieta always had a tale worth telling at the end of their trip.   One time in the mountains they camped for the night in a tent.   Toward dawn Anchieta went out to pray as usual in the open country. When he returned to the tent he took something from the store of provisions and threw it outside.

"There, my little ones!   Take your share!" they heard him say.

"Whom did you give that to?" they asked.

"To my companions."

Next morning in front of the tent they found the footprints of two panthers.   While Anchieta prayed they had sat by his side, then followed him home.

The natives were easily attracted by the elaborate ceremonies and ritual of the church, by the processions, the banners with mysterious words on them, the gorgeous priests' robes, the drums and flutes which made them want to sing and march and dance. The crude magnificence of the churches filled them with awe. Religion to them meant a series of delightful entertainments full of mystery and emotion. Sometimes they were allowed to vary the monotony of their work-a-day lives by a holiday, which "appeared necessary to the missionaries, as well to preserve the health of the Indians as to keep up among them an air of cheerfulness and good humor." Besides all these attractions the Jesuit settlements were the only safe refuges from the plantation owners who wanted slave labor. No wonder, therefore, they flourished mightily!

During these years of his wanderings Anchieta constantly exerted his influence to keep the peace between the Portuguese and the powerful tribes of Tamoyo Indians who had formed themselves into a confederation to drive out the settlers, and forever put a stop to their slave-hunting. With an immense war fleet of canoes, each one formed of the trunk of a single tree, they attacked and ravaged Portuguese villages. Young Anchieta and two other Jesuits volunteered to enter the territory of the Tamoyos and propose plans for a truce. Fearless and unarmed they marched straight into the haunts of the enemy, and stayed there two months while negotiations were in progress. The chiefs consented to the truce and Anchieta remained with them three years longer as a hostage, pledging with his life the good faith of his countrymen.

Sometimes the Indians grew restless and wanted to

break the truce. Those were crucial moments for the young Jesuit.

"Prepare thyself," they told him one day; "satiate thine eyes with the light of the sun, for we are determined to make a solemn banquet of thee."

"No," said Anchieta calmly. "You are quite mistaken. The hour of my death has not yet come."

With prayer and good works he filled his days, and gradually the Indians became his friends. "The Tamoyos narrowly watched the conduct of the holy young man," says one writer, "and the contrast between his manners and their own filled them with wonder and admiration. They looked upon him as something come from heaven and they loved him exceedingly because in their illnesses he taught them the use of different remedies; in addition to all this several prodigies were witnessed by them, which tended not a little to exalt him in their estimation."

In his boyhood Anchieta had made a vow to the Virgin to illustrate her life in verse. During the years of his captivity he composed nearly 5,000 stanzas in Latin, writing them out on the sand and then learning them by heart, for, "having neither books nor pens, he could only describe the work on the tablets of his memory." This, his "Hymn to the Virgin," is one of the masterpieces of religious poetry.

After his release Anchieta served for two years as chaplain of an army sent by the king to protect his colonies from the Tamoyos. Then the provincial called him back to Bahia, where his boyhood ambition to become a priest, in spite of his crooked back, was fulfilled.

In the midst of a sermon one day after he had returned to São Paulo, Anchieta stopped abruptly and covered his face with his hands. After a pause he seemed to recollect where he was. "Let every one of you recite the Lord's prayer," he said, "in thanksgiving to the Divine Goodness which has this day granted us victory over the Tamoyos." The people were vastly astonished at this revelation, but when the soldiers returned a few days later, it was found that the battle had been won just at the moment when Anchieta halted his sermon.

No one in all the community equaled Anchieta in pluck and energy. The districts where he asked to go on preaching trips were always the most dangerous and exhausting. If any of his flock went astray he would drop everything else and go and search for them. Once when two Portuguese soldiers escaped from jail and with some of their followers went off into Indian territory to stir up trouble, he set off after them to bring them back. On a stream in the wilderness his canoe was overturned in deep water, and though he was too crippled to swim, one half hour after the accident he was sitting safely on the bank— a miracle which his friends never tired of recounting. Anchieta never could tell them afterward just what happened or how he got ashore; he was conscious only of three things, one writer remarks naïvely: "Christ, Mary, and not to swallow any water." An illuminating little comment, perhaps, on the fact that with all his faith in the miraculous, the holy father had considerable common sense of his own to depend upon in emergencies! The story ends with rain coming down in torrents, paths full of rocks and brambles, no sign of shelter or chance for a cozy fire and something to eat, and at last, when the dripping, ragged priest hobbles into their midst, the fugitives straightway repent because they have caused him so much pain, and obediently follow him home.

To the people of São Paulo and São Vicente, Anchieta had become very nearly a saint. The fame of his good deeds, his bravery, his wonderful powers, spread far and wide, and it was not long before he was appointed superior of the Jesuit colony of Santo Spirito, a district about half way between Bahia and São Paulo. Rigid self-discipline by now had become a habit with him. While "thinking on divine matters" he forgot to eat. He slept on the bare boards of his dwelling with his shoes, or perhaps a neat bundle of brambles, for a pillow. The three things he needed the most were a desk, a pen and a horse. The first two he borrowed, for of personal property he wished none; and he refused even the gift of a poor old work horse because it would have been too great a luxury. It suited him better to take his trusty staff and make the rounds of his district barefooted. Day and night he was ready to answer calls for medical aid, though when he was in great pain himself and needed assistance he never could bear to disturb any one, and by

sheer will power forced himself not to call for help.
Yet Anchieta was by no means a doleful sort of person, and discomfort and illness seem never to have
put an edge on his disposition. People loved him for
his gayety and friendliness and the most miserable
old Indian in town would cheer up when the *padre*
came to pass the time of day.

Once when walking with another priest barefooted
through muddy paths, Anchieta said with a simple
earnestness: "Some of our fathers wish to be over-
taken by death in this college or that, hoping thus for
greater security at the last moment and to be helped
by the charity of the brethren; but for my part, I could
not desire to be in a better condition to die, than to quit
life in one of these quagmires, when sent by obedience
to the assistance of my neighbor."

By piety alone Anchieta could never have reached so
high a place in the community life. He was a good
business man, and under him the colony grew and
prospered. It took a clear head and a high order of
executive ability to govern a settlement, with its church
and hospital, its schools, its agricultural and industrial
activities, and its outlying towns with hundreds of
Indians, whose every move had to be directed. The
whole structure depended on the Jesuits in charge.

In the typical Indian village built up by the Jesuits,
each inhabitant had his share in the work of the
colony, and his plot of land. They were all like happy,
contented children whose parents protected them and
amused them and saw to it that they were healthy and

busy. But they had neither initiative nor self-reliance, their religion was grafted rather than deeply ingrained, and they became so dependent upon the guidance of the fathers that when, in the beginning of the seventeenth century, the Jesuits were gradually driven out from Brazil, the Indians fell into hopeless confusion and returned to their old wild life or were snapped up by the slave-hunters, while the neat little villages were left to fall to pieces with neglect. The same process was repeated when the Jesuits centered their efforts in Paraguay and northern Argentina. Town after town was abandoned and the once prosperous Indians scattered, when the entire order was finally driven out from all South America by royal decree in 1769.

One day, so tradition goes, Anchieta was sitting on a log of wood by the hearth fire with an old woman who had sent for him to come and hear her confessions. He was politely offered a stool in place of the log, but declined it. "A far more uneasy seat awaits me than that log," he said. Just then a letter was brought to him, sent post-haste by the provincial, directing him to start for Bahia without delay. It said nothing of the reason for this order, but, with his sixth sense, Anchieta knew. When he arrived he found them preparing to install him as provincial of all Brazil.

For seven years the little hump-backed priest held the highest religious office in the New World, and Jesuit power in Brazil reached its zenith. Then, as he

grew too ill and feeble to lead the active life of an
executive, he resigned, and began on a task of which
he had always dreamed, the writing of a history of
the Society of Jesus in Brazil.

In 1597, just before the power of his order was
broken in Brazil, Anchieta, the noblest product of as
fine and self-sacrificing a band of missionaries as ever
lived, died after forty-seven years of constant service,
dating from the days of his novitiate in the old university town of Portugal. "His body was carried and
accompanied by all the Indians of the converted
hordes, and by hundreds of inhabitants who in two
days traversed, on foot, fourteen leagues," as far as
the little coast town of Victoria in Santo Spirito, his
burial place.

In the years that followed, open war broke out. The
hatred of the Portuguese for the Jesuits, who took
away all their slave labor, reached the breaking point.
The government which, nominally at least, had always
protected the priests, was not powerful enough to
hold back the rising tide of rebellion. To save the
Indians and mollify the plantation owners, negro
slavery had been introduced. It became the most
hideous blot on the tablets of Brazilian history, but it
accomplished neither of the results hoped from it.
The Indian settlements were destroyed, and the raging
Paulistas drove the Jesuits further and further back
into the wilderness toward the borders of Paraguay.

It was the end of the prelude of Jesuit activity in
South America. During the next century and a half

the order flourished in Paraguay and the province
of Misiones—Arcadia, it has been called—a land of
sunshine and plenty, dotted with peaceful little towns
where the missionaries had collected their flocks of
Indians.   Then came the decree which sent the Jesuit
fathers quietly and without resistance out of the country forever, and laid waste all they had built up
through the years.   The crops grew wild, the herds
scattered and dwindled, and a whole race of natives
turned from civilization back to savagery.   "The life,
crafts, and arts of the missions were no more.   The
successors of the Jesuits found themselves flogging a
dead horse."   The spirit of the enterprise had vanished, and the Spanish money-makers who expected
to reap the profits of the missionaries' industry saw
their hopes crumble away.   The old missions, the finest
heritage of Catholic orders in South America, passed
into oblivion.

JOSÉ DE SAN MARTIN

JOSÉ DE SAN MARTIN

(Equestrian Statue in Santiago, Chile)

JOSÉ DE SAN MARTIN

A few years after George Washington had won his last battle and the North American colonies were lost forever to Great Britain, the Spanish colonies in South America likewise began to feel the oppression of their mother country's supervision. The Spaniards as lords of the land held every desirable government position and picked all the plums of trade for themselves; while the creoles, those who had been born in South America of pure Spanish descent, were treated as inferior beings quite incapable of managing the affairs of the country which by inheritance belonged to them.

In Europe a great secret society had been formed by a fiery South American patriot, Francisco Miranda, who dreamed night and day of freeing his country from Spanish oppression. The members pledged themselves to work for this end. Among the initiates of this society was José de San Martin, a native of Argentina, who had been sent to Europe for a military education. He had learned the business of war in every branch of the service during almost twenty years of fighting in Spain and France, and he had watched the greatest generals of the day manipulate their troops until he too was master of armies. Yet he had none of that spectacular brilliancy which a great many people seem to expect of a hero. His associates never dreamed that this silent young man, who did a good deal of thinking and not so much talking, was to be a leading figure in the war for independence in South America.

When, in 1812, San Martin arrived in Buenos Aires to help his country fight for liberty, the sparks of revolution had almost been snuffed out in all the colonies except Argentina. Here the creoles had declared their independence, deposed the Spanish governor and elected their own officials. The first thing San Martin did was to train a model regiment of cavalry to serve as the backbone for an army, and he showed such splendid powers of leadership that in 1813 he was given command of the patriot forces. Peru, of all the colonies, was the most thoroughly Spanish, and it was so hemmed in by mountains and deserts, by fierce Indian tribes and by Spanish strongholds that no attack on its frontier could ever be successful. San Martin had to plan a way to carry the cause of independence from one small patriotic center, Buenos Aires, right into this heart of Spanish supremacy in America. His solution of the problem he kept as secret as possible so that the Spaniards would be taken by surprise, and even his own staff could only guess at what might happen next.

First he asked to be appointed governor of Cuyo, an Argentine province lying at the foot of the Andes, and in Mendoza, its capital, he began to organize his campaign. The people of this province, many of them exiled Chilean patriots, thoroughly hated the Spaniards and, as he had wisely foreseen, made excellent helpers. San Martin, with his persuasive personality, could always make others feel as he did. Wherever he went patriots sprang into existence as if by magic, and now the entire community set to work to help him prepare his army. Even tiny children drilled and carried flags; and the ladies gave their jewels to pay for arms and provisions, worked on uniforms for the soldiers, and made a great battle flag bearing a glowing sun—the ancient symbol of the Incas.

To only one friend did he reveal the magnificent plan he was working out in the shadow of the mountains: "A small, well-disciplined army in Mendoza to cross to Chile, finish off the Goths (Spaniards) there, and aid a government of trusty friends to put an end to the anarchy which reigns. Allying our forces we shall then go by sea to Lima. This is our course and no other." But between San Martin and Chile stretched the enormous snow-crowned Sierras of the Andes! No one had ever dreamed that an army with guns, baggage and horses could cross those treacherous passes, some of them 12,000 feet above the sea, and often too narrow to allow more than one mounted man to pass at a time. No wonder San Martin once remarked: "What spoils my sleep is not the strength of the enemy, but how to pass those immense mountains."

It took just three years for San Martin, using all the resources of his province, to prepare for his task.

This meant drilling his troops, gathering provisions, supervising the manufacture of arms and powder; and planning ahead each move of the army. He gave personal attention to every detail of his plan, from providing portable bridges for use in the mountains, and sledges to carry cannon over the snow, down to hiring the last cook for the commissariat and ordering shoes for every mule in the transport.

His chief diversion during this time was campaigning with chessmen in front of his own hearth fire and many an evening he spent in winning all the games from his friends. He took a fatherly interest in the people, and his quiet kindliness and sympathy were in marked contrast to the tyranny and injustice of Spanish officials. One day a farmer was sentenced for bitterly attacking the patriot cause. There was no room in San Martin's big nature for resentment. With a sparkle of fun in his eye he annulled the sentence on condition that the man supply the troops with ten dozen fat pumpkins. Another day a penitent officer came to him to confess that he had lost at cards a sum of money which belonged to his regiment. San Martin quietly turned to a little cabinet in the corner and took from it a number of gold coins. These he gave to the miserable officer, saying sternly: "Pay this money into the regimental chest, and keep the secret; for if General San Martin ever hears that you told of it, he will have you shot upon the spot."

There were many periods of great discouragement during these years of preparation, when the Royalists

seemed everywhere victorious, but San Martin had
only one way of meeting bad news, to go calmly and
confidently ahead as if nothing had happened. When
word came of a great defeat of the patriots in the
north, San Martin invited all his officers to a banquet,
and after the dessert was served he rose to propose a
toast: "To the first shot fired beyond the Andes against
the oppressors of Chile!" The room rang with cheers,
and from that moment there was never a doubt in the
hearts of his men. They had caught that contagious
enthusiasm from their general which was to lead the
army to victory.

In January, 1817, all was ready. A pen-and-ink
sketch of the route to be followed and written instructions had been handed to each major officer by San
Martin himself. From January 14 to 23 the troops,
in six divisions, started off from different points in the
province to cross the Andes at intervals along the
1,300 miles of unbroken mountain ranges. The time
it would take each to cross had been so accurately
reckoned that on the 6th, 7th, and 8th of February,
the entire army poured forth from the six passes upon
the Chilean plateau, exactly as planned, to find the
Spaniards quite distracted and only half way prepared
for defense. The two main divisions of the army filed
out from the mountains simultaneously and, uniting
on the plain of Chacabuco, defeated the Spanish forces
on February 12, and marched into Santiago, then the
capital, with flags flying. To this day in the great
military schools of the world San Martin's march from

Cuyo into Chile is used as a model of how a campaign should be conducted.

San Martin refused the honors which people now wanted to heap upon him, even the commission of brigadier-general, the highest military honor the Argentine government could bestow. The only reward he seems to have accepted was a life pension for his daughter, Marie Mercedes, which he used for her education. With 10,000 ounces of gold given him by the Chileans for his personal use he built a public library in Santiago. And when they unanimously named him as their governor he flatly refused the position. Neither then nor later did he wish any political office which would not directly help along the cause of independence. Personal conquest, glory and profit had no part in his big plan.

The Spanish troops were expert soldiers and greatly outnumbered the invaders of Argentine. After sending for reenforcements, on March 19, 1818, they defeated the patriot forces at Talca, just outside Santiago. It was reported that San Martin had been killed and his army scattered to the four winds. The city rang with Royalist celebrations. But even as the shouts of *"Viva el rey!"* sounded through the streets, San Martin himself rode calmly into town, drew rein before his own house, and as he dismounted, grimly announced to the excited people that he expected to win the next battle and very soon, too.

With the help of friends in Santiago who showered him with money for supplies, he re-equipped his army and marched out to the plain of Maipo to meet the enemy. As he watched their lines forming for battle, he exclaimed: "I take the sun for witness that the day is ours!" At that moment, it is said, the sun in a cloudless sky rose over the crests of the Andes and shone full in his face. Before sunset the Spanish army was put to rout, and the Patriots, within seventeen days of their defeat, had established forever the independence of Chile.

Before the army could hope to find a foothold in Peru, a patriot fleet must sail up the coast to clear the way. Lord Cochrane, an experienced English admiral, took command of the navy in 1818. His ships swooped down on several towns along the coast of Peru and captured them, and his energy and daring struck terror to the Spanish heart. His fiercest onslaughts were directed against Callao, a seaport, six miles from Lima, capital of Peru and headquarters for the royalist army. By the time then that San Martin's land forces were ready to set out, they had the sea to themselves, and the satisfaction of knowing that the Spanish fleet dared not poke its nose beyond Callao harbor. On August 20, 1820, the United Liberating Army boarded transports at Valparaiso and, under the guidance of Cochrane, sailed for Pisco, a port 150 miles south of Lima. Here San Martin divided his army. A force of 1,200 men were detailed to march northward in a great semi-circle around Lima, and to spread the seed of rebellion through the whole countryside. On the way these soldiers defeated a Royalist detachment sent against them. This success boomed the patriot cause, which already had friends in the neighborhood, and it became so popular that one entire regiment deserted the Spanish camp and begged to be allowed to fight with the newcomers. With the main part of his army San Martin made the other half circle around Lima by sea. Both sections were to meet at Huacho, some 70 miles north of the capital. It was a splendid pageant which sailed in regular order past the port of Callao: first the ships of war flying the scarlet and white flags, designed by San Martin for the new Republic of Peru; then the transports, their decks crowded with eager soldiers. It seemed as if every one in town had come out to stand on the walls and watch the squadron go by.

San Martin had no wish to win battles. He issued this proclamation to his men: "Remember that you are come, not to conquer but to liberate a people; the Peruvians are our brothers." Now that he had shown the Spaniards what they might expect of his army and fleet, he planned to stay quietly in the neighborhood of Lima, and by stimulating the Peruvians with a desire for liberty, lead them to assert their own rights. He formed secret societies which carried the new ideas into every nook of the capital, and through his agents and publications acquired enough influence to cut off the supply of provisions from the city.

Meanwhile Lord Cochrane had put the finishing touch to his naval victory by capturing the *Esmeralda,* the prize ship of the Spanish fleet. His men in fourteen rowboats stole into Callao harbor by night, crept between the twenty-six gunboats which protected the big ship, boarded her before any one knew what was happening, and carried her off right from under the 300 guns of Callao Castle.

The situation in Lima, cut off from supplies by land and sea, where it was treason even to mention the subject of independence, grew worse every day. A merchant, just arrived from independent Chile, compared its capital with Lima. "We left Valparaiso harbor filled with shipping; its custom-house wharfs piled high with goods; the road between port and capital was always crowded with convoys of mules, loaded with every kind of foreign manufacture, while numerous ships were busy taking in cargoes. In the harbor of Callao the shipping was crowded into a corner and surrounded by gunboats; the custom house stood empty and its door locked; no bales of goods rose in a pyramid on the quay; no loaded mules plodded over the road to Lima." Indeed, this visitor concluded, every one in the city was miserable except the donkeys, who presumably enjoyed having nothing to do.

During the first six months of 1821 a truce was declared at the suggestion of the viceroy, who thought that if the situation were explained to the government in Spain some compromise might be possible. There was no such word as "compromise" in San Martin's vocabulary, but he consented to the truce because he knew it meant just so much more time for his cause to win adherents.

During this truce San Martin spent much of his time on board his own little yacht which lay at anchor in Callao harbor, and there he received visitors. An English sea captain named Basil Hall came to talk with him a number of times, and in his *Journal*—as good reading as any story book—the captain tells his impression of the great general. "There was little at first sight to engage the attention; but when he rose and began to speak, his superiority was apparent. He received us in very homely style, on the deck of his vessel, dressed in a big surtout coat and a large fur cap, and seated at a table made of a few loose planks laid along the top of some empty casks. He is a tall, erect, handsome man with thick black hair and immense, bushy dark whiskers extending from ear to ear under his chin; his eye is jet black; his whole appearance being highly military. He is unaffectedly simple in his manners; exceedingly cordial and engaging, and possessed evidently of great kindliness of disposition; in short, I have never seen any person, the enchantment of whose address was more irresistible."

Sitting there at his little table the general explained himself to his friends: "People ask why I don't march to Lima at once; so I might, and instantly would, were it suitable to my view, but it is not. I do not want military renown, I have no ambition to be conqueror of Peru, I want solely to liberate the country from oppression. I wish to have all thinking men with me, and do not choose to advance a step beyond the march of public opinion. I have been gaining, day by day, fresh allies in the hearts of the people."

For a long time Spain had been too busy with her own revolution against monarchy to help her colonies. Neither ships nor advice were forthcoming, and on July 6, 1821, the viceroy hurriedly left Lima with his troops, and took to the mountains. The patriotic army, in a semicircle, settled down on the heights to the north of the city, in plain sight of the residents, but made no move to enter. A few prominent citizens immediately sent an invitation to San Martin to come and protect them from threatened uprisings of the slave and Indian population. The general replied most politely that he would not enter the city as a conqueror; he would come only when the people themselves invited him because they wished to declare their independence. But to protect them, he ordered his troops to obey any directions given them by the officials of the city.

When the people heard this splendid offer they could not believe it had been made in good faith. The great general must be mocking them! They shook their heads suspiciously and solemnly gathered to discuss the matter. Tongues wagged excitedly all night long till at last a bright idea occurred to "a strange little man folded up in an old dingy Spanish cloak, with a broad-brimmed yellow hat, hooked loosely on one corner of his small square head, and shadowing a face plastered all over with snuff which, in the vehemence of his agitation, he flung at his nose in handfuls." This little person proposed that they order a certain troop of San Martin's cavalry to move one league farther away just to see if it would. The messenger who sallied out to carry this order returned to say that the troop had packed up its baggage and moved exactly as ordered. This put the Peruvians in high good humor and San Martin became more popular than ever. A formal deputation invited him with great cordiality to enter the city, and on July 9 the first section of the United Liberating Army marched into the capital of Peru while cheers of welcome rang through the streets.

San Martin himself rode into the city the next evening in his usual simple, informal manner, accompanied by only one aide. The story is told that he intended to stop on the way and rest for the night at a cottage outside the city. Unluckily this retreat was discovered by two admiring friars who made San Martin miserable with their extravagant praises. When they began to compare him with Cæsar he could bear it no longer.

"Good heavens! What are we to do? This will never answer," he told his aide.

"Oh, sir! Here come two more of the same stamp," warned the aide from the window.

"Indeed!" replied the general. "Then saddle the horses again and let us be off."

More praises and compliments were awaiting him in Lima, and the people crowded to greet him. One cold, sedate young priest suddenly forgot his dignity

as he shook hands with the great general and burst
forth with a loud shout of *"Viva! Nuestra General!"*

"No, no," said San Martin, "do not say so; but join
with me in calling: *'Viva la Independencia del Peru!'* "

On July 15 independence was declared, and the
scarlet and white flag waved over a new republic. A
great question now confronted the Peruvians: "Who
shall govern us?" San Martin's policy had always
been that as soon as he had liberated the people his
task was over and they must work out their own plans
for government, as the Chileans had done. But the
creoles in Lima knew as little about organizing a government as they had known how to break away from
Spanish rule. San Martin believed this backwardness
was due to their geographical situation which had
cut them off from outside influences, and that they
needed his help before they could be able to help themselves. He issued a decree which temporarily gave
himself the title of "Protector of Peru." In a proclamation to the people he explained his position:
"Since there is still in Peru a foreign enemy to combat,
it is a measure of necessity that the political and military authority should continue united in my person.
The religious scrupulousness with which I have kept
my word in the course of my public life gives me a
right to be believed; and I again pledge it to the people
of Peru, by solemnly promising that the very instant
their territory is free, I shall resign the command, in
order to make room for the government which they
may be pleased to elect."

By his first act in office, San Martin showed that his
definition of independence was big enough to include
not part but all the people. He wanted liberty for the
slaves in Peru as well as for their masters, so he
declared free every person born after Independence
Day and every slave who voluntarily enlisted in his
army. An English teacher living in Lima during this
prosperous year of 1822 wrote: "I never mentioned
a wish to San Martin that was not granted in the most
obliging manner. After his going away, I scarcely
mentioned anything I wished done, that was not
refused."

The harbor now opened to all the world. Ships
with rich cargoes sailed in and out; the donkeys again
had great loads to carry from the wharfs; and the
shops were filled with inexpensive articles of foreign
manufacture which before this had been rare luxuries.
But in spite of their sudden prosperity the Peruvians
hampered San Martin in his two-fold task of putting
affairs at home in good order and planning for further
military campaigns. As he well knew, the national
spirit which he had aroused might turn against him
at any moment, and he had continually to be on his
guard against uprisings. The creoles grew jealous
and factious at the slightest pretext. San Martin was
after all an outsider and came from a rival republic.
Nearly two thirds of his original army, moreover,
unaccustomed to living so near the equator, had been
ill of fever and were in no condition to fight.

San Martin now looked for help from quite another

quarter. At this time a patriot general named Bolivar had reached the northern frontier of Peru with his army. He was fighting for the cause of independence in the North as San Martin had fought in the South. Here in Peru, these two great Liberators who between them had aroused all Spanish America met for the first time. San Martin, without a thought of possible rivalry, rejoiced in the strength and support so near at hand and planned an alliance which should speedily bring final victory. With great enthusiasm he arranged for an interview at Guayaquil, a province just over the borderline of Peru. Bolivar, however, found the idea of sharing his military triumphs with another not at all to his liking. He "wanted the glory of driving out the last Spaniard," and he received the proposal of an alliance coldly, even though San Martin offered to take a subordinate position. At the end of the interview Bolivar seemed agitated and restless, while San Martin appeared as calm, grave and unruffled as always. That night a banquet was given in honor of the visitor, at which both generals proposed toasts. Bolivar's came first: "To the two greatest men of South America—General San Martin and myself." Then San Martin, there at the table of the man who had failed him just as the completion of his career was in sight, again showed the quality of his patriotism. "To the speedy conclusion of the war," he cried; "to the organization of the different republics of the continent; and to the health of Bolivar, the Liberator of Colombia!"

The only comment San Martin seems to have made on his interview with Bolivar was contained in a message to his friend O'Higgins: "The Liberator is not the man we took him to be." Without a word to any one of all that had happened, he decided simply to give up his career and leave Peru. If he remained it would mean civil war between himself and Bolivar who would always be intriguing against him. The cause of independence must not be threatened by quarrels between two rivals. No matter what people said of him he knew he must never tell the real reason for his going, because his own men would turn against Bolivar when they ought to help him. His friends must now be Bolivar's friends. His own career, even his good name, were of small importance compared with the fortunes of the republic. From Lima he wrote his decision to Bolivar: "I have convened the first congress of Peru; the day after its installation I shall leave for Chile, convinced that my presence is the only obstacle which keeps you from coming to Peru with your army."

For the next few weeks he worked hard to leave things in order. First he put his army in the best possible condition for service, and drew up a careful plan of the campaign in which he would have no other share. Then, on September 20, the representatives from the liberated provinces of Peru met, and before this new congress he took off his scarlet and white sash, the emblem of authority, and resigned his office. "I have witnessed the declaration of independence of Chile and Peru," he said in his farewell address; "I hold in my

hand the standard which Pizarro brought over to en-
slave the empire of the Incas. My promises to the
countries in which I made war are fulfilled; I gave
them independence and leave them the choice of their
government."

San Martin had only lame excuses to give for his
sudden departure, such as: "My health is broken, this
climate is killing me;" and on retiring from office, "My
presence in Peru now after the powers I have wielded
would be inconsistent with the dignity of Congress
and with my own." He was accused of cowardice,
and of deserting the republic at the time of its greatest
need. No one thought of blaming Bolivar. Not until
years later when San Martin's letters were published,
and the true reason for his going became known, were
the shadows cleared from his name.

On the night of the 20th he rode away from Lima
as quietly as he had first entered it, and boarding his
yacht at Callao sailed for Chile. But there was no
longer a place for him in South America, even in his
own province of Buenos Aires, for he despised the
small civil wars in which the Argentines were always
entangled. So, besides career and honors and reputation, he gave up home and country.

In a little house on the banks of the Seine near Paris,
San Martin spent many quiet years with his daughter,
reading till his eyes grew too dim, caring for his
garden, absorbed in his trees and flowers. He died on
August 9, 1850. In his will he left his sword—there
was very little else to leave—to the Argentine Dictator.

It was an expression of the deep interest and eager hopes with which he had followed the fortunes of his country to the very end of his life. His last wish came true and is now written upon his tomb in the cathedral of the Argentine capital: "I desire that my heart may rest in Buenos Aires." Statues have been erected to him in the three States to which he gave his services, and to-day he is honored as the greatest of all their men.

San Martin was a good winner. When he won a victory he used it for the glory of his people and the success of his cause, not for his own fame. He was a good loser—there never lived a better. Just before he left Peru for the last time he sent a message and a present to Bolivar. The message read: "Receive, General, this remembrance from the first of your admirers, with the expression of my sincere desire that you may have the glory of finishing the war for the independence of South America." The present was a war horse, the thoroughbred which San Martin himself might have ridden at the head of the victorious patriot armies.

BOLIVAR

SIMON BOLIVAR

BOLIVAR

One day on the royal tennis courts at Madrid an alert, athletic lad, brimming over with nervous energy, won all the sets from his host, the young heir to the throne of Spain. It was the first battle between two men whose armies a few years later fought each other in a long and bitter war; for the lad, Simon Bolivar, led the revolution for independence in the northern colonies of Spanish America, and the prince afterward became King Ferdinand VII whose countrymen Bolivar whipped from coast to coast. While San Martin's armies were carrying liberty from Buenos Aires through Chile to Peru, a similar revolt against the tyranny of governors sent over from Spain broke out in Venezuela, spread through New Granada, or Colombia as it was called later, through Quito, afterward named Ecuador, and finally concentrated in Peru.

"The well-informed party in Venezuela," one writer explains, "the rich, the illustrious, sought independence and sacrificed themselves for liberty; but the people, no!" The prominent, ambitious Creoles had most to gain by a change in government. Their heads were full of republican ideas imported from the mother country, and in Caracas, capital of Venezuela, they held secret meetings and energetically fanned the anti-Spanish feeling which led to civil war. To this party of radicals belonged Simon Bolivar, member of an aristocratic Caracas family. So ardent and impetuous a patriot was he that long before the time was ripe for revolt he had leaped to his feet during a banquet and proposed a toast to the "independence of America," right in the presence of the Spanish governor himself.

Bolivar had always been accustomed to doing and having everything he wanted; never had there been a restraining influence to check his tempestuous, self-willed nature; for his parents died when he was still a small child, leaving him to run wild on the big country estate where he lived; and his little seventeen-year-old Spanish wife lived only a few months after he had brought her home. He was used to an active, outdoor life and spent more time in hunting and riding, swimming and sailing, than in studying with his tutor. This tutor, Simon Rodriguez, however, was the strongest influence in Bolivar's life, for he filled the boy's mind with his own enthusiastic belief in a republican form of government. He dreamed of a day when the Creoles should be free from their enforced dependence upon arbitrary, avaricious Spanish governors, and humiliating subjection to hundreds of absurd little laws made away off in Spain by men who understood nothing of the problems of the South American people. Bolivar was brought up on these teachings and he never forgot them. When, like most rich young Creoles, he was sent to travel in Europe, he had a chance to see for himself the workings of the French Republic, and he admired it so much that he made a vow when only twenty-two years old to be the liberator of his country.

Venezuela was the first colony in Spanish America to declare her independence. Until 1810 no open action was taken. Then, when the news came that the French armies were occupying Spain and that Ferdinand had been deposed in favor of Napoleon's brother, the radical party in Caracas immediately demanded the resignation of Spanish officials, declared "the right of the provinces of America to rule themselves," and appointed its own governing committee, or junta, which should control the affairs of the "United Provinces of Venezuela." The first Congress was convened in 1811, and on July 5, the Spanish colors were torn in small pieces, and the flag of the new republic, stripes of yellow, blue, and red, formally adopted.

Here was the signal for civil war. The rebellious colonies, came the word from Spain, must be subdued at any cost. "I do not know to what class of beasts the South Americans belong," remarked one angry Spaniard. "If the Americans," said another, "complain of having been tyrannized over for three hundred years, they shall now experience a similar treatment for three thousand." Of these same South American "beasts" a great Spanish general reported, a few years later: "Twelve pitched battles, in which the best officers and troops of the enemy have fallen, have not lowered their pride or lessened the vigor of their attacks." That was the spirit of Simon Bolivar. The whole war for independence was like a great pendulum swinging back and forth. On every other swing things looked black for the patriot cause, and then, out of hopelessness and defeat, Bolivar would rise as undaunted and self-confident as ever, mass his troops together, and hurl them madly at the enemy over and over again.

When, in 1812, all the brave hopes of the struggling little Republics were dashed to pieces and every one else had completely lost heart, Bolivar saw his chance to realize the two supreme desires of his life. One was the sincere wish to win independence for his country; the other a selfish ambition to keep for himself the entire glory of doing it. In a few months' time he rose from the inconspicuous position of a volunteer officer, who has been ignominiously defeated at his first action, to be a brilliant military ruler. First he went to Cartagena, the one province of New Granada which had declared its independence, and offered his services. With the few men given him he fought his way toward the borderline of his own State. On the way he heard that just across the Andes in Venezuela a royalist army was preparing to march upon New Granada. He was only a minor officer, with not more than 400 men, and he had had almost no military experience. Without waiting to ask permission, without plans or preparations, he marched across the mountains and rushed upon the unsuspecting enemy. So energetic was the

attack that the royalists, 6,000 in number, were perfectly sure a huge army confronted them and they
beat a speedy retreat. Delighted at Bolivar's success
the Cartagena junta gave him more troops, but
prudently ordered him to pause before going any
farther.

Bolivar refused to be held in leash. He saw a possible rival in a Venezuelan patriot named Santiago
Marino, who had won a few victories on the east
coast, and in a frenzy lest Marino get ahead of him
and reach Caracas first Bolivar went right on with his
whirlwind campaign across the State. On his own
responsibility he issued a terrible proclamation: "Our
kindness is now quenched, and as our oppressors force
us into a mortal war, they shall disappear from America, and our land shall be purged of the monsters who
infest it. Our hatred shall be implacable, and the war
shall be to the death." He began to date his letters:
"Third year of Independence and first of the War to
the Death." Years later he greatly regretted the spirit
of this ferocious declaration and urged instead
"humanity and compassion for your most bitter
enemies."

On August 6, 1813, he entered his native city as
he had dreamed of doing, hailed on all sides by "Long
live our Liberator! Long live New Granada! Long
live the Savior of Venezuela!" He was flattered and
fêted to his heart's content. "A multitude of beautiful young women . . . bearing crowns of laurel,
pushed their way through the crowd to take hold of

the bridle of his horse. Bolivar dismounted and was almost overpowered by the crowns cast upon him. The people wept for joy." He was now "far more powerful than any sovereign living in the world, in proportion to the country and the resources of the people."

But instead of attending strictly to the business of fighting, Bolivar wasted time in enjoying his new honors and establishing himself as Dictator. Even while he was having the inscription "Bolivar, Liberator of Venezuela" placed over the entrances of all public offices, the royalists were recovering their wits. Out on the plains, or "llanos," lived a wild, uncivilized race of cattle breeders called Llaneros, who were magnificent riders and recklessly brave fighters. Boves, a fierce and brutal Spanish leader, won their allegiance by the promise of large booty, and formed them into an army of invincible cavalry, teaching them "the secret of victory, which was to have no fear of death, to go straight on and never look behind." Bolivar's little force was driven from pillar to post by the terrible Boves till in 1814 once more the patriots had hardly a foothold anywhere in Venezuela. Though the Liberator had some devoted followers, like the man who had written him: "General! If two men are sufficient to liberate the Fatherland I am ready to accompany you," yet he was continually opposed by jealous patriots who were loath to obey orders. He never minced words with such enemies: "March at once," he repeated his command to one of them;

"there is no other alternative to marching. If you do not, either you will have to shoot me, or I shall infallibly shoot you." These rivals now took advantage of his failures, and even his admirers turned against him. Betrayed on all sides and denounced as a traitor, he was fairly driven from his country. But in this hour of complete humiliation he stood proudly and confidently before the people and made a farewell address: "I swear to you that this title (Liberator) which your gratitude bestowed upon me when I broke your chains shall not be in vain. I swear to you that Liberator or dead, I shall ever merit the honor you have done me; no human power can turn me from my course."

Then Bolivar returned to New Granada, where he had one loyal friend who still believed in him, Camilo Torres, president of the Republic. "As long as Bolivar lives," he declared, "Venezuela is not lost." The revolutionary junta appointed him Captain-general of the army, and invented for him another of the impressive titles he loved so much: "Illustrious Pacificator." On this occasion Bolivar made a speech in which he boasted that the army of New Granada "would break the chains of all the oppressed peoples of South America."

King Ferdinand, who had won back his throne, now sent 10,000 trained soldiers under General Morillo to put a stop once and for all to the revolutionary antics in which his stubborn colonies were indulging. While this army was landing in Venezuela, in 1815,

Bolivar was quarreling bitterly with a rival Republican leader, Castillo, governor of the independent province of Cartagena, who refused to join the confederation of New Granada. Instead of uniting against the common enemy, the two wasted their time in petty intrigues, till Bolivar, in a wild rage, laid siege to Cartagena, the strongest fortress on the continent, with only one small mounted gun. Then he suddenly realized the absurdity of his position and, as Morillo's army swept over New Granada, he gave what was left of his army to Castillo and resigned. Still undaunted by failure, and never admitting that he himself could be at all to blame, he had a parting shot to fire as usual: "Cartagena prefers her own destruction to the duty of obedience to the Federal Government." Then, with his mind still full of plans for renewing the war, he took refuge on the island of Haiti.

While Bolivar was in exile, the Llaneros were so attracted by the bravery and fair play of a patriotic guerilla chieftain named Paez and so angry at the brutal tyranny of Boves and other Spaniards that they changed their minds and came over to the patriot side. Their successes on the plains of Venezuela put new energy into the revolutionary movement, and Morillo came hurrying back from New Granada in alarm. At this crisis Creole officers had to admit that only one man was great enough to head the revolution, and they petitioned their Liberator to come to the rescue. Bolivar had never left off working desperately to restore the republic, but his expeditions from Haiti were failures. Other patriot refugees intrigued against him and he had narrowly escaped assassination. Now, at the end of 1816, he reappeared among his countrymen, the commander-in-chief of their army, and as confident and enthusiastic as though he had never been scorned and jeered at and defeated.

The Creole army resembled an armed mob rather than a disciplined body of soldiers. One of Bolivar's officers wrote: "There was much to be done to transform these peasants into soldiers and give them a martial aspect. Nothing could be less military than their clothes: a hat of gray wool with a broad brim and a low crown; . . . and an immense square blanket of coarse wool, with a hole in the middle for the head to pass through, hanging from the shoulders to the knees, giving the impression of an armless man." Many carried no arms, except pikeheads fastened upon short sticks, for it was difficult to teach them "to handle a musket, or to fire it without shutting both eyes, turning the head to the rear, and so causing much greater danger to themselves and their fellows than to the enemy!" Bolivar himself cut a strange figure among his ill-assorted soldiers. He loved to be conspicuous. During one battle he wore a jacket and pantaloons of scarlet decorated with gold lace. On another occasion he "was dressed in a green spencer with red facings and three rows of buttons; on his head was a dragoon's helmet, which had been sent him as a sample; he wore Llanero gaiters, and carried in his hand a short lance with a black pennon

adorned with a skull and cross-bones, under which might be read the inscription, 'Liberty or Death.'"
One writer says: "There was nothing heroic in his appearance; he was short in stature, thin and narrow chested; . . . his large black eyes were sunk deep in their orbits, and sparkled with unsteady light, indicative of his character. He looked like one possessed of a latent fire, a man of feverish activity."

He had a tremendous personal influence over his men. In spite of brusque manners and a terrifying temper he was always impulsively generous. One day an officer complained of being robbed of his baggage. Bolivar was unable to recover it, but at once gave him half of his own clothes, which were few enough.

During the next two years Bolivar's position was desperate; yet without funds or arms or supplies he plunged fiercely ahead. Though the Republic had hardly a leg to stand on, Bolivar issued the most optimistic of proclamations. To the people of New Granada he announced: "The day of America has come. No human power can stay the course of nature guided by Providence. Before the sun has again run his annual course altars to liberty will arise throughout your land."

The constant turmoil in which Bolivar lived and the intensity of his feelings wore upon his health. Sometimes he became so excited that he hardly knew what he did. He would expose himself "in the most reckless manner wherever the fight was hottest, seeming to court death as some expiation of the errors he had committed." During one battle, when everything seemed lost and the Spaniards were plowing their deadly way among his little handful of soldiers, he leaped from his horse and dashed into the ranks, shouting to his men that he would die with them. He had many hairbreadth escapes. One time he and his staff were attacked as they slept in their hammocks in a wood. All night Bolivar wandered about on foot alone till he was finally picked up by his own retreating troops. Another night he jumped from his hammock just in time to spoil the plans of some spies who had been sent to murder him, and seized a mule on which to escape. The mule kicked him violently, but a negro soldier came to the rescue with a horse, and Bolivar dashed away hatless and coatless.

By 1818 Bolivar had learned, from his own failures and predicaments and from the example of San Martin, that if he wanted results he needed disciplined troops. He hired skilled European soldiers who had fought in the Napoleonic wars, and to his own ragged, plucky Creole army he added these trained, sophisticated warriors, who looked, in their brilliant and varied uniforms, "more like a theatrical troupe than a body of soldiers going on active service."

When the rainy season of 1819 set in and it looked as though further campaigning would have to be postponed, the patriots held only the valley and low plains of the Orinoco River in Venezuela. Bolivar, always straining to be off and after the enemy, now evolved a stupendous scheme for an offensive attack. He

meant to take his new army through a pass in the
Andes which led right into the heart of Spanish possessions in New Granada and at one blow reconquer
the whole territory. This mountain route was considered impassable and the Spaniards never dreamed
of guarding the other end. In torrents of rain and
most of the time wading up to their waists in water,
the soldiers marched across trackless plains to the
foot of the great range. Several squadrons deserted
on the way. One of Bolivar's officers wrote of him:
"He was very active, himself setting the example of
labor, and frequently working harder than any common soldier. On passing rapid rivers where there
were no fords, he was constantly to be seen assisting
the men over, to prevent their being carried away by
the force of the torrent; and carrying on his own
horse ammunition, arms, and pouches. Whenever, in
short, there was any obstacle to be overcome, he was
constantly on the spot, both directing others and af-
fording the example of his own personal exertions."
During the march through the pass over one hundred
men and all the animals died of exposure. With this
mere skeleton of an army, reinforced by New
Granadian soldiers, Bolivar pounced upon the Spanish
troops, and on August 7, in less than two hours, won
the decisive battle of Boyaca. He had kept his word
to the people of New Granada, and a few days later
he entered their capital, Bogota, in his usual spectacular fashion, a crown of laurel on his head.

Besides carrying the responsibility of the entire

campaign on his shoulders Bolivar had been constantly working to establish what he considered an ideal government. He believed that the republics could never be strong unless they were united. He had set his heart on a federation of Venezuela, New Granada, and Quito as one Republic, called Colombia, with himself as president. When the Venezuelan Congress heard that he had gone to recover New Granada without any authority, it branded him as a traitor and appointed another general-in-chief; when news of the battle of Boyaca came, Congress meekly fell in with his wishes, consented to the union of the three States, and elected him president of the Republic of Colombia. He was given entire control of the army and power to organize as he pleased other provinces which he might liberate. But Bolivar's insatiable ambition wanted more than this; he dreamed of a life presidency. Strange paradox of a patriot fighting, as Washington fought in North America, for political liberty and representative government, and at the same time coveting for himself all the privileges of a king except, as he called it, "a seat on the four crimson-covered planks which are styled a throne!" The sturdy republican representatives of Colombia, however, calmly ignored this undemocratic proposition, and Bolivar was so sensitive to public opinion and so conscious of his own inconsistency that he never tried to force his extreme views upon any congress.

In 1820 King Ferdinand was again deposed, and the new liberal government in Spain tried to make terms with Colombia during a six months' truce. Bolivar used this breathing space very profitably by recruiting troops which were soon going to show the Royalists just what kind of "terms" they might expect. For, only a year later, Bolivar could at last salute his army, as it passed him in review after the great battle of Carabobo in Venezuela, with the words: *"Salvadores de mi patria!"* Again he entered Caracas in triumph, hailed as *El Libertador,* the title which, six years before, he had publicly sworn to deserve, or die.

The circle of liberated colonies was now almost complete. Separating Bolivar and Colombia from San Martin and Peru were the provinces of Quito and Guayaquil. Part of his army Bolivar sent against Quito by sea, under General Sucré. He himself marched south. Between him and Quito lay a buzzing hornet's nest of Spanish troops under a general who confidently promised to destroy the Liberator's approaching army. "That will not be difficult," he was told, "for you have forces equal to Bolivar's and hold impregnable positions." Spurs of the Andes sheltered the Spanish lines, and to make an attack Bolivar would have to cross the unprotected plain of Bombona, leading to a ravine whose one bridge was covered by the enemy's artillery. "Well," remarked Bolivar, "the position is formidable, but we cannot remain here nor can we retreat. We have got to conquer and we will conquer!" As his army advanced, rank upon rank was almost completely destroyed, till when night came on he called upon his last reserve battalion, named *"Vencedor en Boyaca"* because of its bravery at that battle. *"Battalion Vencedor!"* he cried. "Your name alone suffices for victory. Forward! and assure our triumph!" As the full moon rose over the plain, word came that the enemy were in retreat. Sucré's army meanwhile had liberated Quito and the way was now open for another of Bolivar's triumphal entries.

Bolivar then fixed his covetous eye upon the little independent province of Guayaquil and succeeded in reaching its capital ahead of San Martin who wanted to annex it to Peru. He completely cowed the junta by a defiant note: "Guayaquil knows that it cannot remain an independent State; that Colombia cannot give up any of her legitimate rights; and that there is no human power which can deprive her of a handbreadth of her territory." So, as the Department of Ecuador, Quito and Guayaquil were added to the elastic Republic of Colombia. Foreign nations now recognized the Republic, and the Liberator addressed a bulletin to the people, full of the flowery language he loved to use in public: "From the banks of the Orinoco to the Andes of Peru the liberating army, marching from one triumph to another, has covered with its protecting arms the whole of Colombia. Share with me the ocean of joy which bathes my heart, and raise in your own hearts altars to this army which has given you glory, peace, and liberty."

After San Martin had retired in his favor, Bolivar tackled the problem of Peru. The liberating soldiers from both north and south, he told Congress at Lima, "will either conquer and leave Peru free, or all will die. I promise it." But the Royalists held most of Peru, the people were apathetic and afraid to assist the Republicans openly, troops deserted, and ambitious patriots seemed to spend all their time in plotting against each other, till Bolivar finally wrote to a friend: "At times I lose all heart. . . . It is only love of country which recalls the courage lost when I contemplate the difficulties. As soon as obstacles are overcome in one direction they increase in another." One day a messenger came to him at his headquarters with the news that the president of Peru had turned traitor and that the patriot garrison of Callao Castle had mutinied. Bolivar was just recovering from a serious illness, from which he had been unconscious six days, and he sat in a rocking-chair in an orchard, his head tied up with a white handkerchief. He was deathly pale and almost too weak to talk.

"What do you think of doing now?" asked the messenger.

"Of triumphing," replied Bolivar, and the hopelessness of the situation seemed to revive him.

He sent to Colombia for reinforcements, and his letter shows how his impetuous disposition had been tempered during the years: "The interests of all America are at stake; nothing must be trusted to probabilities, still less to chance." In July, 1824, Bolivar's Colombian lancers won the battle of Junin in three quarters of an hour. Not a single shot was fired during the entire engagement, but the victory was so complete that the Spanish general, Canterac, retreated five hundred miles! By 1826 Callao, the last and most stubborn fortress in South America, surrendered. Bolivar's name was famous all over the world. "His feats of arms," San Martin had said, "entitle him to be considered the most extraordinary character that South America has produced; of a constancy to which difficulties only add strength." He had fought in more than four hundred battles in the course of twenty years and he had won the freedom of South America, as he once vowed he would.

What Bolivar could not do was to create a normal, orderly, popular government for his countrymen. He made a great political mistake when he tried to weld a number of States, each inclined to be jealous of the other, into one harmonious Republic. They resented his summary methods. What was the use of getting rid of Spanish government if they were not to be allowed to rule themselves as they pleased? When Bolivar began to plan the union of Colombia, Peru, and Bolivia—the latter named in his honor—into "the Grand Confederation of the Andes," with himself as supreme authority, rebellion gradually spread through all the north. Venezuela first withdrew from Colombia, and Bolivar was forbidden ever to return to his native State. Ecuador also became a separate Republic. The Congress of Colombia took away his military power because for two years he had managed the affairs of Peru, a foreign State. A pan-

American Congress which he attempted to convene in Panama—the first one ever held—was a failure, as well as a prophecy. On every hand were plots against him. Yet his personal prestige was still immense, and if he could have been in a hundred places at once he might never have lost his hold upon the people. One of the very men who schemed for his overthrow wrote: "Such is his influence and such the secret power of his will, that I myself, on many occasions, have approached him in fury, and, merely on seeing and hearing him, have been disarmed and have left his presence filled with admiration."

He felt keenly his failure to unite the Republics to which he had devoted his life. "I have plowed in the sand," he admitted bitterly, and discouraged and heart-sick at the anarchy and disorder on every side, he assembled his last Congress at Bogota. His message ended with this plea: "Compatriots! hear my last word on the termination of my political career. In the name of Colombia I beg, I pray you to remain united, in order not to become the assassins of your country, and your own executioners." His resignation was accepted, and as the "first and best citizen of Colombia," so decreed by Congress, he retired to the country on a government pension, for all his wealth had long ago gone to help the patriot cause. Physically and mentally Bolivar was utterly worn out by his years of incessant campaigning, and by his deep disappointment. "Independence is the only good thing we have gained by the sacrifice of all else," he said in his last

public address. In 1830 he died, only 47 years old.
"El Illustro Americano"—the simple title has been
added to all his others. He had driven the last
Royalist from the land and given the countries of
Spanish America, after all their years of bondage, a
chance to make their own way upward among the
Republics of the world.

JAMES THOMSON

THE CATHEDRAL, LIMA, PERU

(Around Which Centered Much of the Bible-Selling
Activity of James Thomson)

JAMES THOMSON

By the brisk tap of his ruler or a toot on the whistle attached to his watch-chain young schoolmaster Thomson would bring his class of one hundred boys to order every morning promptly at ten o'clock to begin the day's program of "readin', writin', and 'rithmetic." In all Buenos Aires this was the only school where a poor man's son could afford to go, and James Thomson, a Scotchman, had been sent all the way from London by the English and Foreign School Society, in the year 1818, to start it and others like it in South America.

At the beginning of the nineteenth century an English boy named Joseph Lancaster, although he had almost no money and less education than a high school boy of to-day, opened a little school in his father's house and taught all the children in the neighborhood without requiring any tuition fee. When the classes grew too large for him to manage all alone, he trained his oldest and brightest boys to be teachers themselves and hear the recitations of the smaller children. Early each morning he would hold a special class for his monitors, as he called them, and teach them the lessons which they in turn were to teach that day. Lancaster's experiment was so successful that in the United States and in many countries of Europe schools just like his were opened, and he became famous as the inventor of the first public school system.

Thomson's business was to establish Lancasterian schools. But he had still another errand in South America. As an agent of the British and Foreign Bible Society he had charge of distributing and selling Spanish Bibles and New Testaments wherever he went. These two projects fitted together very conveniently, for under the popular new school system the Bible was the chief textbook for all reading classes, and even the smallest children learned their a-b-c's from Bible stories. Thomson had home lessons printed on large sheets of foolscap paper, and when the children gathered around the family lamp at night to study and read aloud the next day's lesson, their parents listened, and enjoyed the selections so much that they began to buy Bibles. Every day an imposing array of visitors came to inspect the new school, and before they left had usually ordered reading books, curious to see what the children were studying. An old Indian chief, who came to "visit school," bought a Bible and took it home as a great prize to show his tribe. One enterprising gentleman stole a dozen copies because he knew he could get a good price for them. "It's too bad," said Thomson, "but he will be sure to sell them and so they will be put in circulation anyway."

Few of the people of South America had ever read

the Bible, many of the priests knew nothing of what it contained, and it was almost impossible to secure a copy even had it occurred to any one to want to read it. When Thomson arrived in Buenos Aires the custom-house officials frowned darkly upon his boxes of Testaments and hinted that they would have to be examined by the bishop, until he explained that his chief business in their country was to open schools, and that the Bibles were needed for his pupils. This was an "Open Sesame." As he wrote home to his friends: "My prominent object here is the establishment of schools. I freely and openly confess this, and in consequence am everywhere hailed as a friend."

Wherever Thomson went he found encouragement and a warm welcome. He was a Protestant in a Catholic country, but he was too broad and sympathetic to try to force his opinions on other people, and he had a genius for making friends. He met only one priest in all his travels who disapproved of his sale of Bibles, although just a few years later the distribution of Bibles was absolutely forbidden by the Catholic Church. This priest thought that the Scriptures ought never to be sold indiscriminately to any one who wanted a good new book to read. It might be misunderstood, particularly if no notes were added to explain difficult passages. Thomson and the priest became good friends and spent many an evening amicably discussing their differences of opinion.

As soon as his own school with all its branches in Buenos Aires was running smoothly, Thomson accepted an invitation from the officials of the Chilean government. They had been begging him to come and open schools for their young people, and had sent the boat fare for his long journey around the cape. In 1821 he left his classes in the care of a priest who had been his right-hand man, and sailed in the brig *Dragon* for Valparaiso.

In those days, when South Americans were fighting for their independence, they felt a newly awakened ambition for the privileges so long denied them by the Spanish ruling class, and the first thing they wanted was schools. An editorial appeared in the Chilean press a few days after Thomson had landed, under the title of "Public Education":

"Ignorance is one of the greatest evils that man can suffer, and it is the principal cause of all his errors and miseries. It is also the grand support of tyranny, and ought, therefore, to be banished by every means from that country which desires a liberty regulated by laws, customs and opinion. . . . The only way we can form an acquaintance with great men is *by reading*. The happy day is now arrived when the infinitely valuable art of reading is to be extended to every individual in Chile. Our benevolent government has brought to this place Mr. James Thomson, who has established in Buenos Aires elementary schools upon that admirable system of Lancaster. . . . He is going to establish schools on the same plan in this city, from which, as a center, this system will be spread through all the towns of the state. There is therefore no obstacle in the way for every one in Chile to obtain education."

Governor O'Higgins of Chile, San Martin's friend and ally, was the leading spirit in all public enterprise. He met Thomson with the greatest enthusiasm, and reserved for his use the largest classroom in the University of Santiago. Within two weeks two hundred children were enrolled in the first school. "They are docile and agreeable," wrote Thomson. "I have just been interrupted by one of my scholars who has called upon me and brought me a ham, a present from his mother."

All the important men in the city were interested in the new schools and liked to visit Thomson's classes. With General O'Higgins as president, a School Society was founded in Chile, and a little printing office opened so that primers and lesson books, especially prepared by Thomson for the children, could be published for home reading. There were no shelves in the public libraries packed with books for young people, no low tables covered with children's magazines. There was almost nothing for them to read, and Thomson often wished that he had a large publishing house as a part of his school system.

In 1822, the year when San Martin was living quietly in Lima, Thomson left his schools in Chile in good running order, and went to Peru to begin his work there. With a letter of introduction he called on the great general. "Next day, as I was sitting in my room," he says, "a carriage stopped at the door and my little boy came running in, crying, 'San Martin! San Martin!' In a moment he entered the room accompanied by one of his ministers. I would have had him step into another apartment of the house more suited to his reception; but he said the room answered very well and sat down on the first chair he reached." Then they talked over the subject of schools. San Martin could hardly do enough to help. A convent was given Thomson for his headquarters. On the Saturday after his arrival the friars who lived in it were ordered to move to another house; by Tuesday they had gone and the keys were in his possession. The huge dining-room was promptly remodeled to serve as a schoolroom with places for three hundred children, and in a few days the school was well under way.

The Patriotic Society in Lima coöperated with Thomson in establishing the schools, and all expenses, including his salary, were met by the government. Every one treated him so cordially and expressed such interest in his work that he predicted a glorious future for South America. He believed that in another decade or two her republics would outstrip many European nations. "I do think," he wrote, "that never since the world began was there so fine a field for the exercise of benevolence in all its parts."

Then came a turning point in the history of Peru. The first Congress met to draw up an outline of the new constitution. The whole city buzzed with speculation about the clauses which might or might not be inserted, and groups of gesticulating people stood on the street corners, till it looked like an election day in New York. The clause of state religion was the chief bone of contention, and Thomson was always on the spot when it was debated in Congress. One man proposed that the clause read: "The exclusive religion of the state is the Catholic Apostolic Church of Rome." Since all South Americans were then Roman Catholics anyway, the only Protestants were foreigners like Thomson. The whole question then was whether foreigners should be allowed to worship as they pleased.

"But," said one member of Congress, "why such ado about toleration? Who is asking for it? Or who stands in need of it? We ourselves do not need any such thing, and foreigners who are here seem very little concerned about the subject. It was not religion that brought them to this country, but commerce. Give them money, therefore, in exchange for their goods, and they will seek nothing else."

A white-haired old gentleman on the committee rose and said: "Gentlemen, this is the first time I have risen to speak in this house, and it is not my intention to detain you long. I understand that the grand and principal features of our religion are these two: to love the Lord with all our heart and strength and to love our neighbor as ourself. . . . Now I ask whether foreigners residing amongst us are to be considered our neighbors or not. If they are, then we ought to love them. Gentlemen, I have nothing further to add."

One fierce old senator demanded again and again that Roman Catholicism be the only religion tolerated in the country. The majority agreed with him. The clause for toleration was voted down. In those few dramatic moments Peru bound herself for almost half a century to the policy which has kept her lagging behind other nations, even other South American republics, and has retarded her intellectual, spiritual, and commercial development. The article finally inserted in the constitution was this: "The Roman Catholic Apostolic religion is the religion of the state, and the exercise of every other is excluded."

Among Thomson's best friends and helpers were the priests. Protestantism was then such a minute influence in the land that the church had hardly begun to fear its power. One bishop who had voted against the proposed toleration clause afterward learned to know Thomson well, and told him that he had always supposed Protestants to be unfriendly to any kind of religion, and that the article finally adopted was only a safeguard against scoffers, such as the men who had written books on atheism printed in England and France and sold in South America. Thomson pointed out to him just how Congress had cut off its own nose by inserting the clause: "Your law prohibiting the public religious exercises of those who differ from the Catholic Church does not hinder atheists from settling in this country, as these have no form of religion they wish to practise. It serves only to prevent the coming of those men who are sincerely religious and moral, and who would be of great use to the country by bringing into it many branches of the arts as well as manufactures."

In 1823 war broke out again, and the Spanish army, 7,000 strong, crossed the Andes and descended upon Lima. The administration "judged it most suitable to remove from the scene of military operations," and the patriot army retreated to Callao. With an old friend, a priest of the cathedral of Lima, Thomson escaped to an English vessel lying in Callao harbor, and after waiting several days for a possible opportunity to return to his school, he sailed for Truxillo in northern Peru where thousands of patriots from Lima had already gone. "I supplied myself with some dollars from a friend," he said afterward, "as I had left Lima without money and with scarcely any clothes other than those I had on."

As long as he had to be away from his schools Thomson planned to make good use of his time by traveling along the banks of the Amazon to visit the Indian tribes living there. Just as he had bought a complete stock of glittering brass buttons, needles, scissors, knives, ribbons, and fish-hooks with which to win the good opinion of these natives, word came that the Spaniards had evacuated Lima. Thomson acted decisively, took the first boat back, and reopened his school.

The longer the war continued the poorer the people grew. "This war rivets the attention of all, and devours all the resources," Thomson wrote in a letter.

During the month when they held Lima the Spaniards had destroyed or confiscated property worth $2,000,-000, and business everywhere was sadly crippled. The city which had once been the richest in the world was now the poorest. The work of the schools was hampered. Some of the older boys dropped out because their parents feared they might be seized on the way to school by recruiting parties and forced into the army. Some of the children had to stay at home because they had no shoes to wear. The government which had pledged Thomson's support became too poor to pay his salary. With prices higher than they had ever been he found himself utterly destitute and hurriedly prepared to leave Lima. Just as he had finished his packing he received a message from the parents of his pupils urging him to stay. They pooled all the money they could spare to pay his salary, and promised to support the school until the government was able to do it.

Thomson had a great vision and a great hope for South America. His chief regret was that, because of the unsettled state of the country, it was impossible to open a girls' school, though a large hall had been selected for it and now stood empty. "The education of women," he declared, "is the thing most wanted in every country; and when it is properly attended to the renovation of the world will go on rapidly." He gave much of his time to translating. For the use of a class of twenty-three men who were studying English he prepared a Spanish-English grammar and

a volume of extracts from great authors. He heard
the story of the Incas and saw the ruins of their empire. Two thirds of the people in Peru were their
descendants and spoke their language, Quichua. With
the help of an officer of the Indian regiment Thomson
translated the Bible for them. For five years he
hunted in vain for a man able to translate the Bible
into Aymara, another native language spoken in Peru.
Then one day after he had returned to London, he
met a stranger in a Paddington coach. The two
chatted a bit together, and Thomson, seeing that the
man was a foreigner, asked him where his home was.
He proved to be a native of the very district in Peru
where Aymara was spoken, and he knew the language
perfectly. Eventually he was appointed to translate
the Bible for his countrymen.

Meanwhile Thomson was selling so many Bibles
that he wrote home: "If I had ten times as many I
am persuaded I could have sold them all." He used
to see shopkeepers seated in front of their little estab-
lishments, spending leisure moments in reading their
Testaments. The priests encouraged it. One showed
his interest by offering to correct the proof-sheets of
the Quichua translation.

Thomson was a great admirer of Bolivar, who, like
the other great men of the day, supported every movement for the betterment of the people. "Bolivar's
weatherbeaten face tells you that he has not been idle,"
Thomson said of him. "No man, I believe, has borne
so much of the burden, or has toiled so hard in the

heat of the day, in the cause of South American independence as Bolivar."

For another year Thomson remained in Lima and then the Spaniards again took possession of the city and he declared he felt as if he had been "transported to Spain." The schools were allowed to go on as usual, but the printing of translations had to be postponed because the printing presses were shut up for safe keeping in Callao castle. Until the government should be restored to order no improvements could be made in the schools, and Thomson decided it was the most favorable time to visit other cities.

His supply of Bibles had been exhausted, and no more had come to him from England, so he started off on his trip with eight hundred New Testaments and one sample copy of the Bible. On the way to Guayaquil his ship called at a small port. "I went ashore to see the place," he said, "and took three Testaments with me. I went into a store near the landing place and being invited took a seat upon a bale of cotton. After some general conversation I opened my treasures, and offered the New Testaments for sale at one dollar each. In a few minutes they were bought. Some little time afterward I was asked if I had any more. I replied that I had but that they were on the ship. I immediately went on board and just as we had got the anchor up a boat came alongside in which I recognized the person who had asked me for more Testaments. He came on board and bought two dozen for which he paid me eighteen dollars."

At another port Thomson went ashore with three Testaments, and was invited to exhibit them in a private house.

"Here," said a neighbor who had come in and was looking at the sample Bible, "here is a book that will tell you all about the beginning of the world and a great many other things."

"I'm not interested in the beginning. I want to know something about the end of it," said another man.

"Then that book in your hands is the very book that will suit you," replied Thomson, pointing to a New Testament. "It will tell you a great deal about the end of the world."

Thomson was a fine salesman, and knew how to advertise his wares. As soon as he reached Guayaquil he had handbills printed which read:

"To be sold at Blank's Store, the New Testament of our Lord Jesus Christ, in one volume, well printed and neatly bound, at the low price of eight *rials*. This sale will continue for three days only, and it is expected that those who wish to procure for themselves this sacred code of our holy religion will improve the occasion now offered them."

At noon these bills were posted. By one o'clock fifteen books had been sold; by the end of the afternoon one hundred and twenty-two had gone. One of the three days of the sale proved to be a holiday, and all stores were closed, but during a few minutes before breakfast when the store had to be opened for some trifle, eleven people came in to buy Testaments. At the end of the third day the receipts amounted to five hundred and forty-two dollars. While Thomson was waiting at the little river wharf for the boat which was to take him on to the next town, he sold over one hundred more Testaments to people who had missed the sale. Then he climbed into one of the passenger canoes which plied along the river and his boxes were loaded in after him. The canoe was the same shape as the usual Indian canoe, but so large that it could hold perhaps twenty passengers. "The South American rivers abound in alligators," he reported. "Great numbers of them lie basking on the banks with their horrible mouths wide open, and when the boat approaches them, they plunge into the river and swim around like so many logs floating about you. At one time I counted alligators, in a very short distance, all at one view and on one side of the river, to the number of forty."

After his river trip the rest of the journey had to be made on muleback. The officials of the towns along the road to Quito treated him with great cordiality. Once when he had taken refuge from a sudden storm in a dreary hut among the mountains, a courier arrived, sent by the governor of the town he had just left, bringing a large hamper of luncheon. The best part of it, Thomson said, was a batch of home-made drop-cakes. He was often entertained at the home of the governor of the town where he happened to halt for the night, and more than once he held his

sale in the governor's own house, where it had all the
festivity of a grand social event.

While riding along an unfrequented road one day
he fell in with a talkative friar and the two ambled
along together. The friar was bound for a Dominican
convent in the next town, and he liked his new acquaintance so much that he invited him to spend the
night at this convent and next day hold his sale there
instead of at a store. Thomson accepted the invitation,
and as soon as the sun rose next morning he posted
his handbills and waited for customers.

"The advertisements were scarcely up," he wrote,
"when one and another and another came tripping in
to purchase a New Testament. In a little the buyers
thickened, whilst the friars stood around enjoying the
sight, and warmly recommending the books to all who
came, and assisted me in the sale when occasion required." In two hours and a half one hundred and
four had been sold. People constantly offered large
sums for the sample Bible. He told them all it was
not for sale, but he sometimes lent it, and he took hundreds of orders to be filled as soon as the publishers
in England could send over a supply. When the
priests in the convent found they could not buy the
Bible they immediately sat down to read it aloud, and
before he left they had promised him to hold a sale
themselves. "We were all pleased with each other,"
said Thomson.

From Quito to Bogota the trail was especially rough
and dangerous. Bandits galloped about over the

countryside and not long before had robbed and murdered some merchants who had been well protected with arms and guides. Of the mountain traveling Thomson said: "You may be said to be riding upstairs and downstairs in these places." Part of the trip was made in a *balsa,* a kind of craft consisting of long poles or trunks of trees laid close to each other, with more poles laid over them crosswise. With its bamboo floor and thatched roof it looked like a little floating house.

Thomson's chief desire in going to Bogota was to found a Bible Society. Three hundred of the most prominent citizens of the city attended the first meeting. The question to be voted upon read: "Is it compatible with our laws and customs, as Colombians and as members of the Roman Catholic Church, to establish a Colombian Bible Society in this capital, as a national organization, whose only object is to print and circulate the Holy Scriptures in approved versions of our native tongue?" The motion was carried almost unanimously. It was decided to hold the meetings in a Dominican convent, and a priest was elected secretary. Catholic and Protestant were working together in harmony to introduce the Bible.

In 1826 Thomson returned to England to make a report of his eight years in South America. "I have no hesitation in saying that the public voice is decidedly in favor of universal education." The elective franchise in Peru had been opened to all men who could read and write. But because the Spaniards had kept the Creoles in ignorance so long, Congress permitted them a little leeway, and the rule was not to be put in force until 1840. Thomson, encouraged by his experiences in Peru, prophesied that by then every one would be qualified to vote!

To-day 75 per cent of the population of South America are illiterate. When the wars for independence were over, the people fell back into their old apathy, the schools declined, the church forbade the use of the Bible. In a few years the results of Thomson's labors had almost disappeared. In Chile the man who had been appointed to superintend the schools returned to England for his health; there was no firm hand to manage the system and it was finally abandoned altogether. After Thomson had left Peru, Bolivar decreed that a central school be opened in the capital city of each province of the state, and a number of young men were sent at the expense of the government to receive the best possible education in England to fit them as teachers. But Bolivar's influence was waning and there is no record that anything came of his plan. The Lancasterian system reached a premature end of usefulness and disappeared with nothing to take its place. The church, the mightiest power in the state, reached out to crush the initiative of the people, and the priests followed the Spaniards as tyrants in the land. They no longer bought Bibles. They burned them in the public squares.

Thomson's eight years made a slight oasis in the barren history of Spanish-American absolutism. It was the time when Protestantism, and the Bible, and religious liberty might have been put there to stay. They were years of wonderful opportunity. The doors were opened a wide crack to let the light shine in and then slammed shut. Progressive forces ever since have been trying to pry them open again. Single-handed, James Thomson labored in the one golden decade of the Continent of Lost Opportunity.

ALLEN GARDINER

ALLEN F. GARDINER

ALLEN GARDINER

When the Inca chieftains of Peru fought their way southward among rebel Indian tribes, they found living in lower Chile a race of men who refused to be conquered. A little later the Spanish invaders made the same discovery. Here were a stubborn, independent people who loved their liberty and meant to keep it. They proved to be as vigorous warriors as the Spaniards themselves, and quick to imitate their weapons and methods of warfare. So great an honor did these Indians consider death in battle that their chiefs had to hold them back rather than urge them forward. One of their generals, when dying, ordered that his body be burned, so that he might rise to the clouds and there keep on fighting with the souls of dead Spaniards. These Indians, "with bodies of iron and souls of tigers," are the Araucanians, the only natives of the Western Hemisphere who were able to resist European invaders. They have always regarded outsiders as beings inferior to themselves, and this racial pride has made them slow to accept modern ideas. "The most furious and valiant people in America," they have been called, and to this day they have kept a large part of their independence.

At the tip end of South America among the islands of Tierra del Fuego, in Patagonia, live some wandering tribes of grotesque, savage, unkempt natives who are considered about the most degraded and repulsive specimens of the human race. Instead of an articulate language they speak in hoarse, jerky, unintelligible grunts. No vestige of religious belief has been found among them. There is no word, no grunt, in their language to express deity. When Darwin visited this region he declared that these hopeless creatures were lower than many animals and incapable of being civilized.

These two races more than any others roused the interest and sympathy of Captain Allen Gardiner, an English naval officer, as he traveled in different parts of the world; and among them he tried, but failed, to establish missionary settlements. To a man who has sailed all over the globe, big distances grow trivial, and the races of men seem like members of one large family. Captain Gardiner was never a minister or an appointed missionary. When he started out he had no connection with any mission board; he was simply a Christian layman, anxious to hold out a helping hand to the people in the human family who needed it most.

The superficiality of all religious life in the cities on the west coast of South America which he visited while cruising in H. M. S. *Dauntless,* had particularly stirred him to indignation: the harshness and intolerance of the priests; the contrast between the spectacular ceremonies in elaborate cathedrals and the poverty and ignorance of the masses of people. If this was the best specimen of Christianity that the most civilized centers could produce, there would seem to be little hope for the Indians. He appreciated the splendid possibilities of the Araucanians, the fine material going to waste; while for the poor Fuegians, utterly neglected and hopeless, he felt the greatest compassion; he knew in his heart that they were worth saving though it might take a hundred centuries. Some one must plunge in and make a beginning. His plan of procedure was to enter these inaccessible regions, live among the natives, learn their customs and language and win their confidence, and when the way was clear bring in missionaries to found a permanent settlement. He worked on the principle that: "We can never do wrong in casting the gospel net on any side or in any place."

At that time he had no success in rousing a similar enthusiasm for South American Indians among the members of the London Missionary Society. With his own income and the moral support of the Society he went first to South Africa and initiated the Zulu mission. "Poor Captain Gardiner! We shall never see him again," said those people who always look with suspicion upon anything new and novel. With "his clothes, his saddle, a spoon, and a New Testament," he settled down among the natives. "We do not wish to learn it," they told him ominously when he produced his Testament, "but if you will show us how to use the nice musket you may stay." The present of a red cloak put the chief into a most friendly

frame of mind, and for three years the mission prospered until a war between the Zulus and the Boers
drove all white people from the district.

Then with his wife and two children Captain Gardiner went to South America, eager to begin on his own
responsibility a tour of investigation among the
Indians. Traveling was no hardship for him. He was
a born wanderer and explorer. He loved roughing it
in the open: sleeping under the stars, galloping over
the plains to visit some rascally Indian chief, crawling
through mountain passes on muleback, fording treacherous rivers. He was a superb horseman and swimmer.
One time on coming to a river too high to be forded,
he says, "I engaged an Indian to swim across with me,
and away we went, leaning together on a bundle of
reeds. The current was fully four and one half or five
knots, but we gained the opposite side in good style, the
Indians all aghast to see that a white man could swim
as well as themselves."

At Buenos Aires the Gardiners packed themselves
and their baggage into a *galera,* or omnibus, drawn by
five mounted horses, which was to carry them over the
Argentine pampas to Mendoza. The family slept and
did most of its housekeeping inside the galera or by
the side of the road, because the post-houses along the
way, usually miserable hovels with mud floors, were
quite uninhabitable. The main discomforts were the
ragged roads on which the clumsy wagon was "not
merely rocked, but agitated to excess"; and the rain
leaked in upon the family apartment so freely that

Captain Gardiner had to drill holes in the floor to drain it off. One large river had to be forded, and the entire contents of the galera were transferred to a raft floated on casks, while the horses, with the peons on their backs, half swam, half scrambled across with the wagon bumping along behind. There was always danger from wandering Indians who sometimes came galloping down upon travelers, whirling their metal-tipped lassos, and with this possibility to spur them on, the party reached Mendoza in fourteen days, record time.

The next stage of the journey was crossing the Andes on mule-back. The procession which ambled forth from the town began with a piebald mare on a leading string with a jangling bell around her neck. The mules liked the sound of this bell and it kept them from stopping to browse. After the seven baggage mules came the children in panniers, one on each side of a mule, led by a mounted peon. Captain and Mrs. Gardiner in the rear kept a watchful eye on the whole party. "While ascending the winding pathway which leads to the 'Bad Pass,'" writes Gardiner, "one of the mules had, unperceived by me, been stopped by the *arriero* to have his pack adjusted. Just as we had reached a point where it was impossible for two animals to pass abreast without one of them being hurled down the precipice into the river below, I perceived this liberated mule hastening towards us with apparent determination to pass. So imminent was the danger that the poles were within three or four feet of

Mrs. Gardiner's head, who was riding immediately behind me; in another second a mere twist of the animal's body might have proved fatal. Sliding off my horse, I providentially was enabled as promptly to unseat her as I had done myself; we then crept into a hollow formed by an overhanging rock, and with the children waited in safety until the whole cavalcade had passed by."

The River Biobio bordered the territory belonging to the Araucanians. The commandant of this frontier warned Captain Gardiner that his plan to enter was unsafe, but helped him in every way he could. With a servant and a government interpreter, Gardiner rode to the nearest Indian district, and the first person he met happened to be the chief himself, Corbalan. "He received me with much hospitality," Gardiner wrote in his journal, "and before even a hint was given of any intended present, a sheep was ordered to be dressed and killed for our supper. Before we retired, for which purpose Corbalan ordered a smooth bullock's hide to be spread for us on the floor, much conversation took place around the fire, for besides his two wives and other members of his family, some men from the neighborhood had joined the party. Corbalan was informed of my desire to acquire his language, in order that I might impart to his people the knowledge of the true God, as also of my wish to obtain his consent to bring my family and reside in his immediate neighborhood. Such a purpose seemed altogether strange to his ears; still he made no objec-

tion, and after some further explanation, he seemed
to enter cordially into it."

The next morning neighboring chiefs arrived by
invitation to welcome the newcomer. Two of them
presented him with boiled fowls. "Where to bestow
this unexpected token of friendship in my case was
rather puzzling; the interpreter, however, at once
relieved me of my dilemma by depositing them in his
saddle-bag." Then Captain Gardiner produced some
colored handkerchiefs and brass buttons and returned
the compliment. A few days later he selected a site for
his mission-house. "But," he says, "I had no sooner
pointed it out to Corbalan than it became evident that
his mind on this point had undergone considerable
change. . . . He plainly acknowledged that, notwithstanding what he had said before, he must withdraw his consent. His neighbors, a large and warlike
tribe, would be offended; they would not permit a
foreigner to live so near them, for as soon as they
heard it they would attack him, and he should not be
able to resist them."

In four other districts and the island of Chiloe
Captain Gardiner made every effort to get permission
to settle. The chiefs were friendly, but either preju-
diced against him by the Catholic friars, or fearing
that he had some ulterior motive in coming among
them, they refused everywhere to let him stay. In one
place the chief told him that he had never allowed a
stranger to live among his people, but in this case he
would make an exception on condition that he be pre-

sented with a bar of salt and a pound of indigo. Afterward when Captain Gardiner had rented a little cottage in the village, moved all his furniture into it, set up the bedsteads and prepared everything for his family, the old chief abruptly informed him that in one moon's time he would have to go. This meant repacking all his possessions and carting them back to the frontier, for it was not worth while moving his family for one month's stay. Another chief "quite laughed at my design of passing forwards to visit some other chiefs beyond. No Spaniards, he said, were living in these parts; they were not permitted to remain."

He wrote to a friend: "Having at last abandoned all hope of reaching the Indian inhabitants where they are most civilized and least migratory, my thoughts are necessarily turned towards the south. . . . Happily for us the Falkland Islands are now under the British Flag. Making this our place of residence, I intend to cross over in a sealer, and spend the summer among the Patagonians." Patagonia was a land of which a Spanish captain in the 18th century reported that "he had surveyed all . . . without finding one place fit for forming a settlement upon, on account of the barrenness of the soil."

The government station on the Falkland Islands was small and dreary, but the people welcomed the Gardiners and helped them build a little wooden house on the barren, treeless shore. The weeks went by and no regular sailing vessel came which could take the Captain over to Tierra del Fuego. Finally the master

of a rickety old schooner agreed to make the trip for
£100.

The first encounter with the natives was discouraging. Two of them appeared on the beach to meet their
callers. "Each had a bow and quiver of arrows. They
spoke loudly and made very plain signs for their visitors to go away. . . . They received the presents
which were offered them, such as brass buttons, a clasp
knife, and a worsted comforter, and condescended to
sit down with what seemed a kind of sullen resolution
not to relax their features or utter another word."
On making a second landing the party found a more
responsive tribe. As soon as they had pitched their
tent, the natives with grim curiosity, moved their own
tents, seventeen of them, with all their belongings,
into a row behind Captain Gardiner's where they could
watch proceedings, and in two or three hours had
transferred their whole village. Gardiner met here
a friendly chief named Wissale and a woolly-haired
North American Negro, Isaac, who could speak English. He explained his errand, how he wished to live
with them in order to teach them good things out of
the Book which he had brought. Wissale was agreeably impressed with this program, enjoyed the refreshments served him, and replied: "It is well. We shall
be brothers."

So peaceable were the natives and so friendly was
the cheerful old chief that Gardiner joyfully began
to plan for a mission-station. With his family he
returned to England to collect funds, but he met with

little response. The missionary organizations were not prosperous enough to undertake the business, and the popular feeling about South America seemed to be: "It is the natural inheritance of pope and pagan; let it alone." It was not till three years later that he could at last carry out his plan. A new organization named the Patagonian Missionary Society, now known as the South American Missionary Society, was formed for the purpose by Gardiner, with the help of men who had caught the contagious spirit of his enthusiasm. But by that time it was too late; the golden opportunity had passed. When Gardiner reached the Strait of Magellan once more, bringing a missionary with him, he found that Wissale had lost his wealth and prestige, an unfriendly chief was in power, and the padre in a new settlement not far away had begun to teach the Patagonians to become "Catolicos." Against this com-bined hostility of natives and white men no Protestant mission could have made headway.

When the two missionaries who had set out with such high hopes returned home again to report com-plete failure the members of the Society were naturally discouraged. Not so Captain Gardiner. He was a quick, impatient man, so intensely active that when the way seemed closed in one direction he would hurry off on some other enterprise without delay, that he might not waste time where so much had to be done. "Whatever course you may determine upon," he said, "I have made up my own mind to go back again to South America, and leave no stone unturned, no effort untried to establish a Protestant mission among the aboriginal tribes. They have a right to be instructed in the gospel of Christ." Paying his own expenses and those of a young assistant, he sailed back to America, and there selected another desolate, neglected territory for his investigations, the interior of Bolivia. "There is not a single mission in the Chaco, and the whole country is before us," he wrote home.

One after another he visited eleven Indian villages. Each chief received him cordially, and to each he made his request to be permitted to live among them. He explained that he was no Spaniard, but belonged to a friendly nation; he promised never to take their land, but to support himself, pay for everything he wanted and bring presents for the chiefs. Eleven times he was refused on one pretext or another. By the time the two travelers reached the frontier again, they were too ill with fever to explore any further. "We have traveled 1,061 miles," wrote Gardiner, "on the worst roads perhaps in the world. We cannot fly about here as in Chile." After repeated efforts, permission was secured from the government to establish a mission on condition that no proselytizing be done and that the work be carried on among Indians only. With the way thus opened Gardiner went to England to urge that a missionary be sent at once. Just at the time, however, when two Spanish Protestants were about to open the Mission under the auspices of the Society, revolution broke out in Bolivia and with a change in government the attempt had to be abandoned.

It had been a long, disheartening series of failures for Gardiner, but with tireless energy he went ahead with new plans. The cautious committee of the Patagonian Missionary Society failed to dampen his enthusiasm, and he toured through England and Scotland lecturing on the need of a mission among the Fuegians. Often it was difficult to collect an audience. The aborigines of South America were too remote to arouse popular sympathy. On one occasion when a lecture had been widely advertised, Gardiner arrived at the hall, hung up his maps, and waited. Not a soul appeared. On the street, as he walked away afterward with the maps under his arm, he met a friend who inquired if it had been a good meeting.

"Not very good, but better than sometimes."

"How many were there?"

"Not one," said Gardiner, "but no meeting is better than a bad one."

Though his personal magnetism won him many warm friends on this trip, the funds contributed were not sufficient to provide for the expedition he had planned. He proposed, however, to use the money as far as it would go. With four sailors, one ship's carpenter, one decked boat, a dingey, a whaleboat, two wigwam huts, and supplies for six months, he sailed, in 1848, for the Strait of Magellan on board the *Clymene* bound for Valparaiso. The little outfit proved pitifully inadequate; the boat should have been twice as substantial to withstand the squalls of that region, and on the first exploring trip was almost swamped.

Gardiner erected his huts on Picton Island. Immediately the Fuegians gathered to watch this remarkable performance, and play mischievous pranks on the white men. One seized a large inkstand and with malicious glee poured its contents over the memorandum Captain Gardiner was writing. They showed alarming partiality for anything they could carry away with them, even the ship's biscuits which had been hidden in a kettle, and articles disappeared so rapidly and mysteriously that the exploring party had to return to the boat to save their property. "A mission vessel moored in the stream must be substituted for a mission house erected on the shore," decided Gardiner after this experience. It meant returning to England, raising more money, and trying to convince the Society that more thorough equipment was essential.

The committee appointed to consider his proposition decided that they could give him nothing but their permission to go ahead, providing he could find the money. An interested woman gave him £700; he himself added £300. With his nautical experience he realized all too well that the little party which finally sailed for Tierra del Fuego a second time was poorly prepared and he warned his companions of all the dangers they must expect. The alternative was abandoning the expedition indefinitely. In 1850, a steamer bound for San Francisco gave them passage: Richard Williams, surgeon; John Maidement, a catechist; Joseph Erwin, the ship's carpenter; three Cornish fishermen, and Captain Gardiner. Supplies for six months were provided, arrangements completed for the delivery of more provisions later, and the two launches, *Pioneer* and *Speedwell,* built for use among the islands, "were the admiration of all nautical men who saw them." They were, however, better suited for use on the Thames River than on the tempestuous Strait of Magellan.

By the end of one month the *Pioneer* was wrecked. The hostility and thievishness of the natives wherever the party landed drove them to take refuge in a retired bay, called Spaniard Harbor, while they waited for the relief party. Their launch seemed like a toy on a big ocean, and Dr. Williams, in his journal, wrote emphatically: "We are all agreed that nothing short of a vessel, a brigantine, or a schooner of 80 or 100 tons burden can answer our ends, and to procure this ultimately the captain has fully determined to use every effort. Our plan of action now is to rough all the circumstances which it may please God to permit to happen to us, until the arrival of a vessel; to take with us some Fuegians, and go to the Falkland Islands, there learn the language, having acquired it, and got the necessary vessel, to come out again and go amongst them."

At Picton Island where they had arranged for the relief ship to land, they buried bottles containing directions: "We are gone to Spaniard Harbor, which is on the main island. We have sickness on board; our supplies are nearly out and if not soon relieved we shall be starved." White stakes with black crosses showed where the bottles were buried, and on the rocks Captain Gardiner painted "Gone to Spaniard Harbor."

But the weeks passed by and no vessel came. It was difficult to catch fish, the supply of powder gave out, and on a steady diet of pork and biscuit, most of the men became seriously ill. "All hands are now sadly affected," wrote Dr. Williams in June. "Captain Gardiner, a miracle of constitutional vigor, has suffered the least, and if I listened to his own words he is still none the worse but his countenance bespeaks the contrary." For days they lived on a fox which "had frequently paid them visits during the night . . . making free with whatever came to hand, pieces of pork, shoes, and even books. To the great mortification of Mr. Maidement his Bible was amongst the latter which being very handsomely bound in morroco was doubtless a booty to the hungry animal!" In July Gardiner wrote: "We have now remaining half a duck, about one pound of salt pork, the same quantity of damaged tea, a pint of rice, two cakes of chocolate, four pints of peas, to which I may add six mice, the latter are very tender and taste like rabbit." Even seeds were made into broth, and rockweed boiled down into jelly.

Gardiner, Maidement and one of the fishermen lived in the wrecked *Pioneer,* drawn up on the beach and covered with a tent, while the other men remained in the *Speedwell,* anchored at the mouth of a little river a mile and a half distant, out of the reach of storms. As they grew weaker it became difficult to make the trip back and forth between the boats. Toward the end of August Gardiner wrote: "One and another of our little missionary band is gathered by the Good Shepherd to a better inheritance, and to a higher and more glorious appointment. Our lives are in his hands, and he can raise up others, far better qualified than we are, to enter into our labors." Not a word of complaint, alarm or impatience appears in the journal which Gardiner kept almost to the last hour.

On August 30, the entry is: "Wishing to spare Mr. Maidement the trouble of attending upon me. . . . I purposed to go to the river, and take up my quarters in the boat. Feeling that without crutches I could not possibly effect it, Mr. Maidement most kindly cut me a pair (two forked sticks) but it was no slight exertion in his weak state. We set out together, but I soon found that I had not strength to procced, so I was obliged to return." Alone in his boat dormitory Gardiner wrote farewell letters to his family. To his wife he said: "If I have a wish for the good of my fellowmen, it is that the Tierra del Fuego mission may be carried on with vigor." During those last few days he worked feverishly on the "Outline of a plan for conducting the future operations of the mission," and an "Appeal to British Christians in behalf of South America," anxious lest he might grow too weak to finish them. One day in the early part of September Maidement retired to a cavern which had been used for sleeping quarters when the tide was not too high. He never returned. Gardiner, the last survivor of the seven, still kept his journal. "He left a little peppermint water which he had mixed, and it has been a great comfort to me," reads the entry, "for there was no other to drink. Fearing that I might suffer from thirst, I prayed that the Lord would strengthen me to procure some water. He graciously answered my petition, and yesterday I was enabled to get out, and scoop up a sufficient supply from some that trickled down at the stern of the boat by means of one of my india rubber overshoes." The next day the journal ended.

Afterward on the shore was found a penciled note, torn and discolored and partly illegible:

Yet a little while, and though . . . the Almighty to sing the praises . . . throne. I neither hunger nor thirst, though five days without food . . . Maidement's kindness to me . . . heaven. September 6, 1851.

Twenty days later the relief ship arrived. Three others were then on the way, sent by anxious friends. The captain wrote in his report: "Captain Gardiner's body was lying beside the boat, which apparently he had left, and being too weak to climb into it again had died by the side of it." After reading the journal, he added: "As a brother officer, I beg to record my admiration of his conduct in the moment of peril and danger; and his energy and resources entitle him to high professional credit. At one time I find him surrounded by hostile natives, and dreading an attack, yet forbearing to fire, and the savages awed and subdued by the solemnity of his party kneeling down in prayer. At another, having failed to heave off his boat when on the rocks, he digs a channel under her, and diverts a freshwater stream into it; and I find him making an anchor by filling an old bread cask with stones, heading it up, and securing wooden crosses over the heads with chains."

To the secretary of the Mission Society in London, Captain Moreshead wrote a sympathetic letter, valuable because it gave the opinion of a hardheaded, practical man: "I trust neither yourself nor the Society will be discouraged from following up to the utmost the cause in which you have embarked; and ultimate success is as certain as the present degraded state of the natives is evident. Their state is a perfect disgrace to the age we live in, within a few hundred miles of an English colony."

Far from discouraging further missionary activities, the story of Allen Gardiner, published far and wide, and discussed all over England, gave great impetus to a lagging cause. "They buried themselves on the desert shore," it was said in a current magazine article, "but all the people of England attend their funeral." Those who had been faintly interested began to do something; those who had been utterly indifferent began to think. The public conscience felt an unaccustomed prick. The Society which Gardiner had founded, now on a sound and permanent basis, and profiting by his experiences, energetically arranged to establish a mission on the Falkland Islands. It was resolved "from thence to hold a cautious intercourse with the Fuegians by means of a schooner named the *Allen Gardiner*." The plans were submitted to experts who recommended that "the vessel be well armed, of from 100 to 150 tons, rigged American fashion fore-and-aft sails, no square ones." Such was the ship launched in 1854, and one of the first volunteers to join the mission party was Gardiner's only son, Allen. On Starvation Beach, Spaniard Harbor, is a tablet bearing seven names. The inscription reads in part:

"THIS TABLET WAS ERECTED BY THE CAPTAIN AND CREW OF A VESSEL BUILT ACCORDING TO THE WISHES OF THE ABOVE-MENTIONED CAPTAIN GARDINER, AND NAMED AFTER HIM ... THE WHOLE UNDER THE DIRECTION OF THE PATAGONIAN OR SOUTH AMERICAN MISSIONARY SOCIETY, TO WHOM THE VESSEL BELONGS, AND OF WHICH SOCIETY CAPTAIN GARDINER WAS THE FOUNDER."

The names of Allen Gardiner, his son and his grandson have all been closely associated with Araucania. At the time of the Society's jubilee in 1894, a special fund for increasing the work among these Indians was raised, and a new and larger mission established in memory of Captain Gardiner. The superintendent of the mission wrote: "Wonderful is the thought that our brave founder tried so hard and failed to gain a footing in this country about fifty years ago, whilst to-day it is our happy privilege to preach the gospel of peace and good-will towards men in camp, village and town throughout the length and breadth of Araucania."

In one of the finest of the histories of the Argentine Republic there is this little paragraph: "The South American Society has done noble work in supplying buildings and chaplains, and the courage and enterprise of the hardy colonists is a striking episode in the history of colonization." Through those who came after him Allen Gardiner finds his place in the history of the continent.

JUAN MANUEL ROSAS

JUAN MANUEL ROSAS

JUAN MANUEL ROSAS

While the South American Republics were still in the making, about one hundred years ago, Juan Manuel Rosas, not yet eighteen years old, managed his father's great stock farm on the southern plains of Argentina. He was a handsome young giant, of an unusual Creole type, fair enough to look like an Englishman, and so strong, daring and reckless that he became the popular idol of the whole countryside.

The people among whom Rosas lived, whose interests he made his own, belonged to one of the most romantic races in the world, the half-savage Gauchos or herdsmen of the Argentine pampas, descendants of European colonists and native Indians. The homes of the Gauchos were the backs of their own cow-ponies, they galloped over the country as they pleased, and clung as fiercely to personal liberty as to life itself. Once a week they rounded up their herds just to keep track of them. The rest of the time they spent in catching wild cattle, and breaking in horses. Like the llaneros of Venezuela, who refused to fight in places where they could not ride and deserted if their horses were killed, the Gauchos did everything on horseback—fishing, hunting, carrying water, even attending mass.

Viscount James Bryce says of the Gaucho: "He could

live on next to nothing and knew no fatigue. Round him clings all the romance of the pampas, for he was taken as the embodiment of the primitive virtues of daring, endurance, and loyalty. Now he, too, is gone, as North American frontiersmen like Daniel Boone went eighty or ninety years ago, and as the cowboy of Texas and Wyoming is now fast going."

Rosas had been born in the city of Buenos Aires, but he loved and belonged to the rough, wild, free life of the pampas and there he grew up. Everything the Gauchos did, he could do a little better; even his feats on horseback were more spectacular than theirs. He would mount a horse which had never before been ridden, and with a gold-piece placed under each knee, let the enraged pony buck under him until it was worn out, without displacing the coins. A favorite performance was suspending himself by his hands from the cross bar of a corral filled with wild stallions; at the moment that the fiercest of these dashed by beneath him, he would drop down on its back and without saddle or bridle ride off over the plains till the horse was tamed. Sometimes he would "dare" a Gaucho to lasso the hind legs of his horse as he rode at full gallop, and as the horse was thrown forward, Rosas, pitched over its head, would land gracefully on his feet.

Few ever lived who could control a band of Gauchos. Rosas managed them as easily as he did an unbroken colt. He was the dominant figure of the region where he lived. To him, the young master of great estates, the Gauchos flocked hoping for employment, and so many came that to keep them all busy Rosas had enormous corn and wheat fields planted. His was the first large agricultural enterprise in South America, and the cultivation of crops as an Argentine industry began from that date.

Those were merry and exciting days for Rosas and his Gauchos. "Every festive occasion, every return of the young patron from a visit to town," so the gossip ran, "was celebrated by fiestas and dances lasting two or three days, when a dozen or twenty oxen were roasted in their hides, and Rosas, of course, always won the palm in the dance and in improvisations on the guitar." But there was plenty of hard work and hard riding done on the estate. Rosas demanded absolute obedience from his laborers, and every rule he laid down for them he was scrupulous in keeping himself. So perfectly disciplined were they that they constituted a small, invincible army, ready to repel all attacks from the dreaded Indian tribes who roamed over the pampas seeking plunder.

Even the Indians themselves fell under the spell of the young leader. One famous chief gave him the title *Cacique Blanco,* or White Chief, because he had so many followers. Years later when Rosas was governor of Buenos Aires, a large party of his old Indian friends came up to the city to pay him a visit. Some of them caught smallpox while they were there, a disease much dreaded by the Indians, for whole tribes had practically been wiped out by epidemics.

Rosas called on an old chief who had it. Then he showed the little mark on his arm to the other Indians, who had deserted their sick friends, and told them how it had enabled him to visit the chief without danger. With the greatest delight and anticipation 150 Indian men and women begged to be vaccinated, proudly regarding the mysterious little pricks as an infallible charm against the evil demon who brought them the disease.

At the age of eighteen, because his parents criticized his management of the estate, Rosas resigned the position, refused to be dependent on them any longer for money or assistance, and started off to make his own way in the world. For a time he worked in Buenos Aires as a cattle dealer, collecting the cattle from various farms and driving them to the city to sell. Then, with a partner who supplied the capital while he contributed brains and experience, he began the business of salting meat for exportation to Brazil and Cuba. This industry up to that time had been unknown. To-day it is an important feature of Argentine trade. By order of the government, which feared a depletion of stock, Rosas was soon obliged to give up his enterprise. But he had now made enough money to buy land of his own, and he became a cattle-farmer down on the Indian frontier, 150 miles south of Buenos Aires.

Here he formed another army of devoted Gauchos and peasants for protection against the Indians. His own peons, called *Colorados* or the Reds, from the

color of their picturesque uniforms, served as a
mounted guard, and a band of friendly Indians were
the vanguard. No one else could have controlled,
much less formed into an efficient military machine,
these wild, undisciplined elements of the plains, yet
without them Rosas might never have become the
great military leader of the Republic. When a bitter
political war broke out in Buenos Aires, he rushed
into the fray at the head of his Gaucho army and
took the city by storm. The administration called him
the "Liberator of the Capital," and he became the
acknowledged commander-in-chief of all the fighting
men of southern Buenos Aires. On returning to his
farm he added to his popularity among the country
people by starting a subscription of cattle to make
good the losses incurred during the outbreak.

Then for several years Rosas remained quietly in
his own district, organizing his independent army
which the loyal Gauchos joined in preference to the
government troops. One of his men who had been
arrested for murder gave as his excuse: "He spoke
disrespectfully of General Rosas, and I killed him."
So successful was Rosas in all dealings with the Indians
that the government commissioned him to fix a new
southern boundary line between Argentina and the
Indian territories. Under his influence many wandering tribes which had been a menace to life and property were induced to settle peaceably on farms.

In 1829 another conspiracy threatened the capital.
General Lavelle of the Argentine army, returning from

a successful campaign against Uruguay, proposed to make himself governor of the province. Rosas with his country militia completely spoiled the general's plans and forced him to come to terms. There was now no further question of Rosas' growing influence. He had become a power to be reckoned with in the affairs of the Republic.

Rosas and General Lavelle were always deadly political enemies, but it is reported that one night the general rode out all alone to the enemy's camp to talk things over. Rosas was not there, so he sat down to wait. "He was tired after his long midnight ride; for many nights, too, he had slept on the ground, and the sight of a comfortable bed was an irresistible temptation; when Rosas returned to his quarters he found his own bed occupied by the commander of the hostile army fast asleep. Lavelle on awakening accepted his enemy's courteous invitation to remain tucked up between the blankets, and in that comfortable attitude he arranged terms of peace with Rosas."

It took the South American Republics a long time to learn how to govern themselves. The policy of Spain to exclude Creoles from sharing in the business of government had left them unprepared. The rising generation hardly knew what it meant not to live in the midst of revolutions. There had been the great war with Spain; wars between the republics; wars between the provinces within a republic; wars between political parties; and wars between ambitious leaders of the same party who tried to oust each other. In

Argentina there had been thirty-six changes of government between 1810, the date of her Declaration of Independence, and 1835, when Rosas became dictator. The strongest and most cruel tyrant kept in power longest. Lawlessness, bloodshed, and murder were commonplaces. It was considered an extraordinary piece of mercy when on one occasion a victorious general ordered only one out of every five of his prisoners to be shot.

Rosas grew up in the midst of revolutions and when he came into power he used the only weapons then in vogue: force, cruelty, contempt of human life. By trampling ruthlessly on every opposing element, he controlled the high-spirited, rebellious republic for seventeen years, and from a half dozen quarreling provinces he whipped it into a solid nation at a time when union of any kind had seemed an impossible dream.

As a reward for his services in defending the capital against Lavelle, Rosas was elected governor of the province for a three-year term. He put an end to civil war by ordering all who rebelled against his administration to be shot without trial. Thus he organized the first substantial government the Argentine Republic had ever known. The legislature loaded him with honors and gave him the title of "Restorer of the Laws." When his term of office expired he declined reelection, because the legislature refused to give him all the power he wanted.

The next year Rosas headed a great expedition

against the wild Indians of the southern pampas who had become so bold and outrageous in their attacks on the country people that no one felt safe over night. They were completely subdued. Twenty thousand are said to have been destroyed, and seventeen hundred captive white women and children liberated. Rosas became more popular than ever—"Hero of the Desert" he was called.

Meanwhile the people of Buenos Aires had been finding out to their sorrow that no one but Rosas could cope with the political situation. Five times they urged him to accept the presidency of the Republic under a national constitution. Before doing so Rosas wisely demanded for himself what other dictators had usurped—an absolute authority, which he urged as necessary for the safety of the State. Into his hands the people of this so-called Republic put "the sum of the public power," and having done so immediately began to hate him and plot against him, as seems to have been the custom in those days. His word was law. If he wanted a man murdered his orders made the murder a legal act.

He used his vast powers to put the various departments of state on a sound basis, and to get rid of all his enemies or rivals. He organized a police and spy system which ferreted out crimes and plots in the remotest corners. No criminal could escape. He put an end to the mishandling of public funds by requiring every official to give an accurate account of all sums received or paid out. During his presidency not one cent was embezzled or lost from the treasury; the employees of the government were paid like clockwork; foreign debts were reduced by a fixed amount each year; and the taxes were lighter than ever before. He encouraged the immigration of peasants who were used to tilling the soil, as an example to his own people, and agriculture prospered so that the country was able to supply its own grain. The cattle industry flourished, for the herds were protected from cattle thieves and Indians, and each owner's brand respected as never before.

Rosas worked as hard as any of his officials to put the public affairs in good order. He personally superintended every department of the administration, working day and night without fixed hours for sleep. He seldom appeared in public, and gave interviews while he walked in his garden. His daughter, Manuelita, was the only person in whom he ever confided. She is said to have been a second edition of her father. He had brought her up like a boy, and she knew so much about national affairs that he often asked her advice on important matters. With her beauty and assumed naïveté, she made an excellent spy on occasion, leading on her poor admirers to reveal political secrets which it would help her father to know.

There had gradually emerged from the tangled Argentine politics two distinct parties, the Unitarians and the Federalists. The province of Buenos Aires had always aspired to being a powerful central government, as Paris in the French Republic, controlling the other provinces. The outlying provinces on the other hand were jealous of her power and wanted a union of states all having equal liberty and privileges, like the United States. Rosas and the Gauchos naturally belonged to the latter party, the Federalists. But during his dictatorship, party lines became decidedly vague, for he at once began to group under the head of Unitarios all who opposed him, no matter what their party preferences. Federalists came to mean Rosas' friends, Unitarians his enemies.

As the Rosista reign of terror began it became an act of treason for man or woman to appear in public without a rosette of scarlet, the Federalist color. Even horses and carriages, houses and shops flew the red flag and bore mottoes with Rosas' slogan: "Long live the Federals! Death to the savage Unitarians!" To be seen on the street without some such mark of loyalty meant suspicion, and suspicion usually meant sudden and violent death. When two harmless ships arrived in port one day from Portland, Maine, loaded with brooms, buckets, and washtubs, the Americans found that their wares could not be sold at any price because they were painted green or blue, the Unitarian colors! A yacht on one of these ships, ordered by Commander Brown of the Argentine navy, could not be received because green and white were its colors. The shrewd Yankee sailors, glad to be obliging, sandpapered off the green paint and laid on two coats of bright vermillion. On the stern, in neat gold letters, they painted the Rosista motto, and then a crew wearing scarlet and white costumes delivered the boat. The next day the rigging of the American ships displayed long red lines of freshly painted brooms and buckets hung up to dry. They were afterward sold at very fancy prices.

In the first part of his "reign" Rosas' position was often desperate. He was fiercely jealous of foreign interference and his high-handed measures led him into trouble with both France and England. For two years the French navy blockaded Buenos Aires, but no nation on earth was big enough to tell Rosas what he ought to do. When the French admiral threatened to bombard Buenos Aires, Rosas replied: "For every ball that falls in the town, I will hang a French resident." His stubborn insistence on Argentine rights won great praise from San Martin and it was to Rosas that he willed his sword.

It is said that the Dictator loved to torment and flout foreign naval officers and ambassadors. Sometimes he would keep them waiting months before receiving them at all. One day when two dignified Spanish officers paid him an official visit in the customary full-dress uniform he greeted them in his shirt sleeves. Another time he boasted that he intended to have the maize for his breakfast porridge pounded by the English ambassador. When the minister was seen approaching the palace Rosas sent his daughter to stand in the entrance-hall and pound the maize in a mortar. The visitor politely took the pestle to help her. Rosas and his retinue then appeared upon the scene. Once when he was requested to reply to an ultimatum in forty-eight hours, he waited twenty-five days before condescending to notice it at all.

Montevideo in Uruguay, on the opposite shores of the Plata River, was the refuge for anti-Rosistas, and from there they stirred up trouble. One of them published an article called: "It is a Meritorious Action to Kill Rosas." Another sent a parcel containing a bomb to the Dictator, purporting to be a valuable collection of historic medals. It lay in his library for two days till Manuelita and one of her girl friends happened to open it. The machinery was imperfect and it never exploded.

Opposition to Rosas was in the air, and it culminated in a huge conspiracy. Some of the plotters were among the most prominent citizens of Buenos Aires. But no one could catch Rosas unawares. He was more than a match for the Unitarians who had kept the country humming with civil war for years. By hospitality and friendliness he liked to lead his enemies on to thinking they had pulled the wool over his eyes. Through his spies he would keep watch of all their little tricks and then turn the tables on them just in time to save himself. On the evening before he knew the outbreak would occur, he invited his friends and his enemies to a wonderful fête in the palace gardens. Among the guests were all those in the conspiracy to execute Rosas next day and confiscate his estates. Within two hours after the last guest had departed that night every one of the conspirators was quietly arrested, brought back to the palace grounds and shot. People heard the steady firing of the guns, but supposed it to be "a parting salute" from Rosas to his guests of the evening—and so it was.

The next morning the citizens were invited to hear a public address by the Dictator. At nine o'clock he appeared on a little balcony of the palace, attended only by Manuelita, who carried a red banner bearing the Federalist motto. Then he told the crowds below him what he had done to rid the country of its greatest enemies, the "savage Unitarios."

At about this time a terrible secret society called the Mazorca Club was formed and there were no more revolutions. Like the Klu Klux Klan it did its deadly work in the middle of the night and few on its black list ever escaped. Men merely suspected of being Unitarians or friends of Unitarians were stabbed in their beds. Tiny red flags, stamped with the signet of the club, which could not be duplicated by non-members, were attached to the victims. People hardly dared whisper to each other the news that "Last night ten throats were cut!" Even women and children were murdered, and no man dared hide when the Mazorqueros called at midnight, for it might mean death to his family instead. Patrols guarded the coast all night to prevent the escape of suspects. One man managed to get away by embarking openly at noon. Another hid in a cellar for twelve years, living on food which his wife smuggled in to him. On the day of Rosas' downfall a pale, white-bearded figure crept up out of the cellar into the sunlight like a ghost.

There were only two men in Argentina powerful enough to be possible rivals of the Dictator. One of these, Quiroga, a far worse tyrant than Rosas, showed signs of having designs of his own. Rosas despatched him to a distant province on an errand. On the way Quiroga and his attendants, even the horses drawing the carriage and a dog inside of it, were set upon and killed by unknown ruffians. The other rival, Vincente Lopez, died shortly afterwards, and it was reported that his physician received a handsome reward from the private purse of the president.

By 1842 Rosas, with the help of his favorite general, Urquiza, had either murdered his enemies, driven them to Montevideo, or frightened them into helplessness. The power of the "savage Unitarios" was broken; people were in a state of sullen acquiescence. He had forced internal peace upon the country. Thomas Dawson says of Rosas during those dreadful days in Buenos Aires: "For political reasons he did not hesitate to kill, and to kill cruelly, but he did not kill for the mere sake of killing." [1]

The first man who dared, without having his throat cut, to defy the Dictator was Urquiza himself, once his friend and staunch ally. Urquiza had been appointed governor of Entre Rios, the most independent of all the provinces; he was a loyal Federalist and

---

[1] *South American Republics.*

anxious that his province should receive fair play. The break between the two men occurred because Rosas, though professing to be a Federalist, lived and ruled like a Unitarian. All the power of the Republic was concentrated in Buenos Aires. From there Rosas dictated laws which gave that city special privileges. He even forbade other cities to engage directly in commerce with outside nations; everything had to be sent to Buenos Aires first and shipped from there subject to duty.

In 1851 Urquiza issued a public decree which declared Rosas to be "a despot who has trodden under his feet the brow of a youthful Republic." With the anti-Rosistas who had fled to Uruguay and some of Rosas' troops who had been besieging Montevideo and deserted, besides his own followers, he crossed the Parana River, which separates Entre Rios from the rest of Argentina. His army of 24,000 men was the largest that had ever been assembled for a South American battle, and their thousands of horses swimming across the river presented an extraordinary spectacle. On February 3, 1852, Rosas was defeated. With his daughter he fled to the British Consulate, and thence they boarded ship for England. It was reported that they escaped to the ship disguised as sailors.

Rosas once said to his grandson long afterward: "I want you to remember what I am going to say. Whenever anything was done over there in my name, but which was not directly attributable to me, I always got the blame for it; anything good and right my enemies always put to the credit of my ministers." Rosas has been called the most bitterly hated man in Argentine history. Even to this day they celebrate the date on which he was finally driven from the country. Monuments have never been erected in his memory, nor public squares named after him. But his hands first shaped the constitution of the Argentine nation, and his cruelty and tyranny brought about a reaction in favor of Republicanism. No one ever wanted another Dictator.

Urquiza, who became the next president, finished the work of consolidation; a Federal Constitution, outlined years before by Rosas, was adopted and is in effect to-day. The Republic began to learn her first lessons in self-government, and the stage was clear for the prosperity and industrial development of modern Argentina.

At the age of fifty-six Rosas, in England, again took up the old life he loved so much, the raising of cattle and breeding of horses. For twenty-five years he lived as a peaceful country gentleman, popular with his neighbors and with his workmen. "No one would have thought," someone used to say, "that the singularly handsome old gentleman who lived quietly and unobtrusively on a little farm near Southampton was the once famous despot of Argentina."

DOMINGO F. SARMIENTO

DOMINGO F. SARMIENTO

DOMINGO F. SARMIENTO

In the town of San Juan, near the foot of the Andes in eastern Argentina, lived a fine old family named Sarmiento which could trace its ancestry back in a straight line to the early colonists. On the mother's side, generation after generation had produced men of remarkable intellectual ability—writers, teachers, historians, bishops. The youngest of the family, Domingo, born in 1811, had all the brilliant talents which seemed to be the inevitable heritage of these people. His relatives were "personages," but they were very companionable ones even for a small boy, and there was never a dull moment in the Sarmiento household. With his uncle, a clergyman who had once been chaplain in San Martin's army, he would spend hours talking on history, politics, and good government, and learning a variety of fascinating things about the world.

"I never knew how to spin a top, to bat a ball, to fly a kite, or had any inclination for such boyish sports," Domingo confessed many years later. "At school I learned how to copy the knaves from cards, later I made a copy of San Martin on horseback from the paper lantern of a grocer, and I succeeded, after ten years of perseverance, in divining all the secrets of caricatures." He especially loved to mold saints and soldiers out of mud and play with them. For the saints he invented elaborate ceremonies of worship; the soldiers he and his young neighbors arranged in two armies, and fierce battles were carried on with wax balls, seeing who could knock down the most figures with the fewest shots.

The family was desperately poor. Domingo's mother—one of those great mothers of great men—had married a man who had no money and never quite succeeded in making any. He worked on a farm driving mules, and did various odd jobs for a living, always dreaming of wonderful projects which never amounted to anything. It was the plucky young mother who built their little home. Before her marriage, although it was an unheard-of thing for a woman of good family to work for wages, she had earned a little money by weaving. With this she hired two peons to build a two-room house on a bit of land, "thirty yards by forty," which she had inherited. She put up her loom under a fig-tree on the grass, and while she wove directed the workmen, sometimes even stopping to help them. Each Saturday she sold the cloth she made during the week and from the proceeds paid the men their wages.

"The sunburned bricks and mud walls of that little house might be computed in yards of linen," Domingo once said. "My mother wove twelve yards per week, which was the pattern for the dress of a friar, and received $6 on Saturday, not without trespassing on the night"—quaintly elaborate Spanish phrase!—"to fill the quills with thread for the work of the following day."

With the picture of his mother always before him Sarmiento had the deepest respect for honest work, whether it was done with the hands or with the mind. He kept as a precious treasure the shuttle, two hundred years old, which his mother, grandmother, and great-grandmother had used. No one appreciated better than he the dignity of manual labor, and that in a day when Creole gentlemen scorned to lift a finger in any kind of industrial work. By her own efforts his mother supported the little family, and though sometimes she hardly knew where the next day's meals were coming from, she never told of her poverty. Her wealthy relatives and her brothers, the parish curates, never dreamed how hard the struggle was.

Each morning at sunrise the noise of the whirring loom would wake the family, a signal that it was time to be up. "Other industrial resources had their place on the narrow territory of twenty yards not occupied by the family mansion," Sarmiento wrote. "Three orange trees shed their fruit in autumn, their shade always. Under a corpulent peach tree was a little pool of water for the solace of three or four geese, which, multiplying, gave their contribution to the complicated and limited system of revenue on which reposed the existence of the family; and since these means were insufficient, there was a garden which produced such vegetables as enter into South American cookery, the whole sparkling and illuminated by groups of common flowers, a mulberry-colored rose-bush and various other flowering shrubs. . . . Yet in that Noah's ark there was some little corner where were steeped and prepared the colors with which she dyed her webs, and a vat of bran, from whence issued every week a fair proportion of exquisitely white starch." Candle-making, baking, and a "thousand rural operations" went on in the busy little household.

"Such was the domestic hearth near which I grew, and it is impossible that there should not be left on a loyal nature indelible impressions of morality, of industry, and of virtue."

Domingo's father was determined that the boy and his two sisters should have opportunities which he himself had missed, and he constantly encouraged them to read and study. "He had an unconquerable hatred for manual labor, unintellectually and rudely as he had been brought up. I once heard him say, speaking of me, 'Oh, no! my son shall never take a spade in his hand!'" He used to borrow learned works—the *Critical History of Spain,* in four volumes, was one of these—and insist that his son read them every word. Long before school-days Domingo had learned to read. His uncle afterward told him that at the age of four he "had the reputation of being a most troublesome and vociferous reader." The first book he ever owned was a Roman Guide Book which he used to pore over by the hour. Sarmiento always said that he was indebted to his father for his love of reading.

When he was five years old he went to school. Argentina's declaration of independence had given her colonists a new pride in themselves, an impetus to educate their children who were going to be free citizens of a free country, and the provincial government had opened a primary school, the first of its kind in San Juan. Before that even the children of wealthy parents received almost no education except what they could pick up at home.

"In this school," Sarmiento says, "I remained nine years without having missed a single day under any pretext, for my mother was there to see that I should fulfil my duty of punctuality under the penalty of her indescribable severity. From a child I believed in my talents as a rich man does in his money or a soldier in his warlike deeds. Every one said so, and after nine years of school life, there were not a dozen out of two thousand children who were before me in their capacity to learn, notwithstanding that toward the end I hated the school, especially grammar, algebra, and arithmetic."

After he had gone as far as he could in the elementary school he studied Latin with his uncle, and mathematics and surveying with an engineer. At fifteen he was teaching a class of eight pupils twenty years old who had never learned to read. A year later he became an apprentice in a merchant's shop, spending all the money he could spare for books and all his leisure in reading them.

"I studied the history of Greece till I knew it by heart, and then that of Rome, feeling myself to be successively Leonidas, Brutus, Aristides. . . . During this time I was selling herbs and sugar, and making grimaces at those who came to draw me from my newly-discovered world where I wished to live."

He read every book he could lay his hands on. Among them were the Bible, a *Life of Cicero,* and two formidable treatises entitled: *Natural Theology and Evidences of Christianity,* and *The True Idea of the Holy See.* He liked them all, and in his imagination lived over and over again the lives of the characters he read about. He loved best the *Life of Benjamin Franklin.* "No book," he said, "has ever done me more good. . . . I felt myself to be Franklin—why not? I was very poor like him; I studied, as he did, to be a *doctor ad honorem!* and to make myself a place in letters and American politics."

Then one day his career as shopkeeper came to a sudden end. "I was told for the third time," he wrote, "to close my shop and mount guard in the character of ensign of militia to which rank I had of late been promoted. I was very much opposed to that guard, and over my own signature I complained of the service, and used the expression, 'with which we are oppressed'!" For this offense Sarmiento was speedily summoned to the presence of the governor. As the boy approached, the governor neither rose in greeting nor lifted his hat. "It was the first time I had presented myself before one in authority. I was young, ignorant of life, haughty by education and perhaps by my daily contact with Cæsar, Cicero, and other favorite personages, and, as the governor did not respond to my respectful salute, before answering his question, 'Is this your signature, sir?' I hurriedly lifted my hat, intentionally put it on again, and answered resolutely, 'Yes, sir.' . . ."

After this bit of pantomime the two eyed each other suspiciously, the governor trying "to make me cast down my eyes by the flashes of anger that gleamed from his own, and I with mine fixed unwinkingly to make him understand that his rage was aimed at a soul fortified against all intimidation! I conquered, and in a transport of anger he called an aide-de-camp and sent me to prison."

"You have done a foolish thing, but it is done; now bear the consequences," his father told him.

Various officials tried to force him to tell the names of people he had heard complain of the government, but he said to them: "Those who spoke in my presence did not authorize me to communicate their opinions to the authorities."

Not long after his release, as the governor was riding through the streets with a train of fifty horsemen, young Sarmiento on a sudden impulse fired a sky-rocket at the hoofs of some of the horses. "We had a wordy dispute," he says, "he on horseback, I on foot. He had a train of fifty horsemen, and I fixed my eyes upon him and his spirited horse to avoid being trampled upon, when I felt something touch me behind in a disagreeable and significant manner. I put my hand behind me and touched—the barrel of a pistol, which was left in my hand. I was at that instant the head of a phalanx which had gathered in my defense. The Federal party was on the point of a hand-to-hand encounter with the Unitario party, whom I served unconsciously at that moment." The governor rode on, worsted for the second time by a mere boy. His spirited rebellion against the tyranny of the government in those dreadful days of revolution and civil war was the cause of these two incidents, and he never hesitated to attack the evils which roused his indignation.

He definitely allied himself with the anti-administration party, the Unitarios, and for the next month gave all his time to studying the political principles of the two great parties of the republic. "I was initiated thus by the authorities themselves into the party questions of the city, and it was not in Rome or in Greece but in San Juan that I was to seek national liberty."

At eighteen he left his shop and joined some troops that were preparing to march against the tyrant Quiroga. He barely escaped being taken prisoner, and finally landed in Mendoza with his father, who followed him everywhere "like a tutelar angel," possibly to restrain his son's hotheadedness. At Mendoza he was appointed a director of the military academy because of his knowledge of cavalry maneuvers and tactics, most of which he had picked up in the course of his reading. Here he discovered one day a French library which inspired him with a great desire to learn French. He found a soldier from France who agreed to give him lessons. By the end of six weeks he had translated twelve volumes. He kept his books piled on the dining-room table except at meal-times, and it was usually two o'clock in the morning before he closed his dictionary and blew out his candle.

No Unitario's life was safe at this time, and the Sarmiento family with many prominent citizens of the province of San Juan were obliged to seek safety in Chile. In Los Andes on the Chilean side of the mountains Sarmiento taught for a time in a municipal school, the first and only one in the town. Then he walked all the way to the coast to accept the position of a merchant's clerk in Valparaiso at a wage of about sixteen dollars a month. More than half of this he invested in learning English, part going to his professor, and ten cents a week to the watchman on the block for waking him at two in the morning for study. He never worked on Sunday, but he made up for this by sitting up all Saturday night with his books and Spanish-English dictionary. After six weeks of lessons his teacher told him that all he needed further was the pronunciation. Not until he visited France and England years later did he have a chance to learn to pronounce correctly the languages he had acquired in six weeks.

Intensely alert for every opportunity of advancement, Sarmiento shortly became foreman in a great mining plant. With all the rest of his duties he managed to read in English one volume a day of all the works of Sir Walter Scott. The Argentine workers in the mine, most of them exiles like himself, used to meet in a big kitchen after the day's work was over to discuss politics. Sarmiento was always on hand in his miner's costume of "doublet and hose," with a red cap and a sash to which was attached his purse, "capable of holding twenty-five pounds of sugar." Whether it had any money in it, as is the habit of purses, no one knows. In these discussions Sarmiento was the court of last resort. The men asked him questions, and strangers who sometimes dropped in to listen were often surprised at the remarkable attainments of this young man who looked in his rough clothes like the humblest peon. He used to draw birds and animals and make caricatures to amuse the miners, and he even gave them French lessons. He had a passion for telling others everything he knew himself, and a marvelous gift for making those he taught eager to learn.

But as time went on he longed to recross the mountain pass which lay between himself and home. Ill and almost penniless he arrived in San Juan to find few of his old friends left there. It happened that the government officials needed an expert to solve a complicated mathematical problem. Sarmiento was able to help them, and gained considerable prestige for his cleverness. He made new friends among the brightest of the young Liberals, and together they began to wake up the sleepy, apathetic, intellectually barren little city with a great variety of activities, in which Sarmiento was always the leading spirit.

Under his direction a college for young ladies was founded. Nothing had ever been done before in the province for the education of women, and Sarmiento wrote a vigorous article setting forth the need of such a school as he proposed. For two years it was his pet enterprise and through it he exerted a very real influence on the community. The energetic little group also started a dramatic society, the first in the country, and invented many public amusements which raised the general tone of society life.

With the help of three of his friends Sarmiento published a periodical named *La Zonda,* which treated of public education, farming, and other topics about which he thought people ought to know. The first two numbers contained nothing to which the government could reasonably object, but it feared what he might say next. The governor on some flimsy pretext fined him twenty-six dollars. When Sarmiento would not submit to such oppressive methods he was marched off to prison. On the advice of his friends he yielded the point for the sake of his school and the affair blew over. But he was wholly unsubdued.

"My situation in San Juan became more and more thorny every day," he says, "as the political situation became more and more charged with threatening clouds. . . . I spoke my convictions with all the sincerity of my nature, and the suspicions of the government closed around me on every side like a cloud of flies buzzing about my ears." It was not long before his fearless articles led to his rearrest, and he was imprisoned in a dungeon designed for the worst political offenders. For months his life was a series of narrow escapes. At one time a howling mob of Federalists in the streets demanded his death, and the governor would have ordered his assassination had he dared.

Sarmiento left the prison to go into exile once more in Chile. *"On ne tue pas les idées,"* "Ideas have no country," he said, and went right on contributing articles to the press. For a time he edited a political journal, then gave it up to found a magazine of his own, the *Nacional.* His vigorous writings on all kinds of subjects thoroughly aroused public opinion and started violent controversies which made men think. There was no greater evil in South America than the indifference of the mass of the people to all questions of public welfare and prosperity. Sarmiento proved a tonic for mental laziness.

When he heard one day that a bitter enemy of Rosas, Colonel Madrid, was in Mendoza preparing to defy the government, Sarmiento turned his back on his editorial desk and determined to return to his own country, and help to fight against the president. Just as they had reached the summit on their way across the Andes, Sarmiento and his companions spied in the distance hundreds of black, hurrying specks coming toward them. Madrid and his men in retreat were taking refuge in the mountains. Their position, without food, shelter, or medicine, was desperate. Sarmiento fairly ran down the mountain side to Los Andes, hired a secretary, invited himself into a friend's house, and for twelve hours worked to save the lives of those Argentine troops. Before the day was over he had sent twelve mountaineers to help the fugitives, bought and despatched six loads of food and bedding, written to the Argentine minister in Chile for government aid, started appeals for charity, arranged an entertainment for the benefit of the soldiers, and written one of his stirring articles to rouse public sympathy. People responded instantly and in three days sufficient food and medicine for a thousand men had started over the Andes.

"My mother brought me up," Sarmiento wrote, "with the persuasion that I should be a clergyman and the curate of San Juan, in imitation of my uncle; and my father had visions for me of military jackets, gold lace, sabers, and other accouterments to match." But from the time when he was a small boy in the government school Sarmiento had known what he wanted to do more than anything else in the world with his life. Many years later, on the occasion of laying the corner-stone of the Sarmiento School in San Juan, he said in the course of his address: "The inspiration to consecrate myself to the education of the people came to me here in my youth."

The idea of educating the common people in schools supported by popular taxes had never occurred to the people of Chile. In Santiago, now that his project of fighting for Argentina had come to an end, he organized primary schools for the poor, and founded the *Monitor for Schools,* a journal for teachers, in which he discussed educational problems. Perhaps nothing he did was more important than raising the profession of teacher to a higher plane. At that time teaching was considered to be not only a humble but an unworthy occupation. A story is told of a robber who had stolen the silver candelabra from a church altar. As punishment he was condemned, not to the penitentiary, but "to serve as a schoolmaster in Copiapo for the term of three years." To this despised profession Sarmiento gave new dignity and importance. He founded the first normal school in either North or South America for the training of men who should make the profession of teaching an honorable one.

One of his students during those years writes of him: "Sarmiento always treated us as friends, inspiring us with that respectful confidence which makes a superior so dear. He was always ready to favor us and help us in our misfortunes; he often despoiled himself of his own garments to give them to his pupils, the greater part of whom were poor. He often invited us to accompany him in his afternoon walks, in order to give us more importance in the eyes of others and to comfort our hearts by encouragement. . . .

He treated his pupils thus, not because we were individually worthy of the honor, but to give importance to our profession, then humiliated, calumniated, despised. He himself, in spite of his learning and his influential relatives, was called by the disdainful epithets of *clerk* and *schoolmaster,* and was insulted every day by the supercilious Chileans!"

After Sarmiento had directed the normal school for three years, all the time continuing his writing, editing, and newspaper work, he was commissioned by the Chilean government to visit Europe and the United States to study school systems. During his travels he met distinguished men in all the large countries of the world, and received honors wherever he went. One interesting result of his trip was a conversation he had with San Martin, in which he learned why the great general had ended his career so abruptly. He was the first one admitted to the secret, and it was through him that the Argentines discovered the truth about their greatest patriot.[1] In the United States he became a friend of Horace Mann, who had first introduced the common school system of education. As soon as Sarmiento reached Chile again, he established this system there.

While he was in exile, he did a large part of the writing which has distinguished him not only as educator and statesman but as a man of letters. Aside from the numerous periodicals he founded from time to

---

[1]See page 57.

time, he published many books, some of them political
treatises, some of them travels, and one, *Recollections
of a Province,* largely autobiographical. Perhaps his
best-known work is a history of Argentina in the days
of the tyrants, called *Civilization and Barbarism,* in
which he poured out all the bitter rebellion in his
heart against the policy of the government.

While Sarmiento was giving so lavishly of his
genius to his adopted country, he stood ready at a
moment's notice to respond to his own country's need
for help. Rosas had decreed a ban of perpetual
banishment upon him, but when Sarmiento heard in
1851 that General Urquiza was preparing to march
against Rosas, he left Chile at once to offer his services. As a colonel he fought in the famous battle
which drove Rosas from the country. Then, seated
at the tyrant's own desk, and using his pen, he wrote
a vivid description of the battle. Six days later he
left the army because he realized that Urquiza had
every intention of making himself another such dictator as Rosas. The minute he decided on this he
wrote a note to the general in which he told him with
his usual uncompromising bluntness that he had chosen
a thorny path which could lead only to disaster.

He began now to take a still deeper interest in
politics, but refused to accept office because he could
not approve of the policy of the government of Buenos
Aires which had refused to join a Confederation of
Argentine Provinces. But he did accept the director-
ship of the department of schools of the municipality

of Buenos Aires. When he began this difficult, uphill work, a resolution was passed appropriating $600 for all the schools in the city! After a year he was granted $127,000 for his department, and with it a splendid Model School was erected. When soon afterward he was elected state senator from Buenos Aires, he immediately proposed that extensive public lands recently held by Rosas should become school property and that school-buildings should be built through all the provinces.

He used his great influence to bring about the final union of Buenos Aires with the Argentine Confederacy, and he made a brilliant address before a convention of provincial delegates, opposing a bill to establish a state religion. It was largely through his influence that absolute religious toleration and liberty of speech were declared legal.

The interests of the people were his first concern in public life. He obtained permission to divide a large tract of land near the capital into small farms, and these he sold cheaply to prospective farmers. In the center of this land he built a "Chicago of the desert," as he called it. Squares and streets were laid out, a church, a schoolhouse, a bank, and a railroad station were built, the whole settlement springing up as quickly as a Western mining town in the United States. Thousands of people went on excursions out to the desert to see the marvelous spectacle. At that time thirty-nine farmers held the land. Ten years later 20,000 people lived in the district, and a railroad was built giving it connection with Buenos Aires.

Soon after this, he returned to his own province as governor. He founded a university; high schools for boys and girls; and primary schools in every section of the province. After the bad governors who had held sway, the people could hardly believe their good fortune! He left this office after a short term to go to the United States as ambassador from the Argentine Republic. While he was there he determined that his country should have the benefit of every progressive idea that the United States could suggest, and through his books and reports describing American education, industries, and institutions, he kept the ruling minds of Argentina in close touch with these ideas. The Argentines were devoted admirers of Abraham Lincoln, and Sarmiento wrote a life of Lincoln which he printed at his own expense and sent to South America for general distribution. He started an important review called *Ambas Americas*—"The Two Americas"—which he hoped would bring the two countries into closer sympathy and understanding—a precursor of the work that is being done to-day to promote the mutual friendship and helpfulness of the continents.

After seven years of absence from home he heard from his friends that he was a candidate for the presidency of Argentina, and they urged him to return at once to conduct his political campaign. This he refused to do. He announced no party platform, gave no pledges, took none of the customary measures to influence the voters in his favor, but remained in Washington quietly attending to his business as usual. In 1868 he was elected almost unanimously. "His election," says one writer, "is said to have been the freest and most peaceful ever held in the republic and to have represented as nearly as any the will of the electors." With his administration the old revolutionary days of the republic vanished into the past, and the period of modern Argentina began in peace and prosperity. Even his opponents admitted that the great Schoolmaster President's administration promoted only the best interests of all the people, their education, their resources, and harmony between provinces which had once fought in bitter rivalry.

After his six-year term was over he served in Congress and shared in every intellectual and moral movement, giving all his best powers, up to the time of his death at the age of seventy-seven, that the people of his country might have a little of all they missed in opportunity and happiness during the terrible years of revolution and bloodshed.

In the midst of all the honors which the grateful Argentines heaped upon their noblest statesman, and the incessant demands of public life upon his time and energy, Sarmiento never ceased to work for what, as a boy in school, he had conceived to be the foundation of national life. "Give me the department of schools," he once wrote to a friend. "This is all the future of the Republic."

DOM PEDRO II

DOM PEDRO II

DOM PEDRO II

It was a strange prank that history played upon the people of South America about a century ago. Just when the Spanish-owned colonies were on the brink of the revolution which made them independent republics, the Portuguese territory of Brazil welcomed to her port of Rio de Janeiro the royal family of Portugal, driven into temporary exile by Napoleon and the armies of France. A royal charter graciously declared Brazil a kingdom, and the king on his recall to Lisbon left his son, Pedro I, as regent. The other colonies fought for fifteen years to become republics; Brazil became a monarchy as a matter of course and a few years later, in 1822, won her independence with hardly a struggle.

Then, instead of running true to form, the monarchy came much nearer being a real republic than its neighbors which, though called republics, were usually under the thumb of military dictators during that chaotic first half century of their independence. Brazil had a constitution, a Congress or General Assembly, a legislature elected by the people; but better than all this, Brazil had for fifty years an emperor who respected the wishes of his people, whose ideals of government were genuinely democratic, Dom Pedro II. General Rosas, president and dictator of the

Argentine Republic, came from the common people and ruled like a king; His Majesty Dom Pedro, with the blood of the Bourbons, the Hapsburgs, and the Braganzas in his veins, administered the affairs of the nation like a president. He was probably the most democratic monarch who ever lived. An American who knew him said: "He was far more democratic, not only in manner but in feeling, than many a self-made millionaire who fought his way from the gutter among the democracy of our own United States."

When he was five years old the first responsibilities of an emperor fell on his shoulders, for old Pedro I, at odds with his ministers, abdicated the throne and left the country. An enthusiastic populace, hailing young Pedro II. with loud "Vivas!" and elaborate ceremonies, installed him emperor. A court-day was appointed in his honor. The excited people unharnessed the horses from the imperial carriage and drew it themselves through the city streets. Then from his little chair in a window of the palace Pedro reviewed the troops of the empire and afterwards received the greetings of his officers in uniform, and of diplomats from all over the world. Next day he went back to his schoolroom, and for ten years a troublesome Regency managed the affairs of Brazil for him.

At last a large political party in the capital grew tired of installing regents and electing new ministers, and insistently demanded that the emperor himself begin to reign, although legally he was still too young. According to the constitution an emperor reached his majority at the age of eighteen, and Dom Pedro was only fifteen. In a speech before the legislature the leader of the party dramatically broke off in the midst of a violent attack against the Regency and cried: *"Viva a maioridade de sua Majestade Imperial!"* The galleries rang with such applause that the speech was never finished. By ten o'clock on the morning of July 23, 1840, ten thousand citizens had surrounded the palace of the Senate, while within, the president of the General Assembly made an announcement which set the whole city wild with joy: "I, as the organ of the Representatives of this nation in General Assembly convened, declare that His Majesty Dom Pedro II. is from this moment in his majority, and in the full exercise of his constitutional prerogatives. Viva Dom Pedro II., constitutional Emperor and perpetual defender of Brazil! Viva Dom Pedro II.!"

So mature was the young emperor in mind and appearance that he was well fitted to play the part of an eighteen-year-old. His tutors were the best that could be found in Europe or South America, and he was a brilliant student. He had a trick of relighting his lamp at night and studying for a while after everyone had gone to bed. Natural history, mathematics and astronomy were his favorite subjects at that time. But in the course of his life he studied almost everything under the sun, and he could talk fluently on any subject in English, German, French, Italian or Spanish; he read Latin, Greek and Hebrew. When he was sixty he learned Sanskrit. His library was packed with histories, biographies, encyclopedias and law-books and he knew so much of what they contained that "a stranger," it was said, "can scarcely start a subject in regard to his own country that would be foreign to Dom Pedro." Besides his library the emperor loved peace, happiness and prosperity; these were his gifts to Brazil during his long reign, while surrounding nations struggled with anarchy and civil war.

Before Dom Pedro was eighteen he signed a contract of marriage with a princess whom he had never seen, Theresa Christina Maria, sister of the King of the two Sicilies. A Brazilian squadron conducted her to Rio, and the city received her with splendid ceremonies. The people were always glad of an excuse for a display of royal pageantry and enjoyed it a great deal better than their unpretentious emperor did.

Dom Pedro kept no court—the formalities would have been irksome—and it is said that he "would gobble through his state dinners in a hurry to get back to his books." An American tells how he met the emperor one day in Petropolis, the summer capital, standing on the street corner by the railroad station with a single attendant, apparently out for a stroll, and stopping when the train came in to see the new arrivals. In Rio he usually drove about in the afternoon bareheaded in a rickety old barouche drawn by four mules, with a book on his lap, reading busily whenever he was not bowing right and left to his friends. When he visited New York he arrived at his hotel carrying a satchel and wearing a linen duster. Always on his foreign tours he dropped his title and traveled as inconspicuously as possible, signing his name simply as D. Pedro d'Alcantara.

An American traveler in Brazil tells of visiting the emperor at the beautiful palace of San Cristoval out in the country five miles from Rio: "His Majesty met me upon an inner corridor of the palace, attended by a single aide-de-camp, who however immediately disappeared. The chamberlain mentioned my name and nationality. His Majesty advancing shook hands cordially, and asked me in well-accented English when I had left New York. The chamberlain with a nod left me alone with the emperor. Dom Pedro II. is a very striking figure, tall, broad-shouldered, erect, with a large, intellectual head. . . . He was simply clad in a black broadcloth 'dress-suit,' and wore on his breast the beautiful star of the Imperial Order of the Southern Cross, and in a button-hole the diamond and gold badge of that grand old historic order, the Golden Fleece of Austria and Spain. His Majesty always wears these decorations, rarely any others, nor is he often seen in uniform or gala dress of any kind. . . . He gives no balls or dinners, and is always accessible to the public once a week, generally on Saturday evenings. He is especially noted for his tact, energy and humanity. He is, therefore, very popular, and much loved by all his subjects."

Once, while touring through the interior of the country, "seeing Brazil first," he was entertained for several days by the leading resident of a certain town.

During the visit he learned from a confidential source that his host was unable to meet a large debt which was soon due. When Dom Pedro was about to say good-by, he remarked casually: "You have forgotten to put away an important paper I have seen in the drawer of the bureau of the room I occupied." It was the receipted bill for the entire debt.

Under Dom Pedro's guiding influence Brazil gained steadily in power, importance and reputation. Home industries and foreign commerce doubled. Telegraphic communications were established with the United States and Europe. Good steamship lines, both coastwise and oceanic, made Brazil accessible to all the world. Public property was opened to settlement, and the government became as hospitable to all foreign enterprise as it had before this been exclusive. The Brazilians, little interested as a rule in commerce, banking, railroading, engineering, needed the stimulation and example of outside influence.

Above all things Dom Pedro wanted to stimulate the love of knowledge among his people, to give the boys and girls of every class an equal chance. Free public schools were established all over the empire. At his request Professor Agassiz, then traveling in Brazil, gave a popular course of lectures in Rio on scientific subjects which the public were invited to attend. Free lectures had never been dreamed of before in Brazil. A raised platform was built in the hall for the use of the emperor, but it stood empty during the series. Dom Pedro preferred to sit among

the audience.   One time the emperor learned that
3,000,000 francs had been pledged by citizens for a
fine bronze statue of himself to be given the place of
honor in a city square.   Dom Pedro, expressing his
deep gratitude, said that it would please him far more
if the money could be used for public schools instead.
The grade and high school buildings of Rio have always been noted for their beauty, size and equipment.

While so many of the South American states were
lagging far behind the times, Brazil, under Dom Pedro,
caught up with other progressive nations of the world.
Liberty of speech and religious tolerance were not
even questioned, but taken for granted.   Indeed if a
man on the streets of Brazil wanted to speak his mind
about any grievance he was quite apt to begin right
on the spot while the crowd gathered to hear him—
the equivalent of a "mass protest meeting" in Madison
Square, New York.   A noted Protestant clergyman, a
friend of many Brazilians and of the emperor himself,
wrote: "It is my firm conviction that there is not a
Roman Catholic country on the globe where there
prevails a greater degree of toleration or a greater
liberality of feeling towards Protestants."   One of the
most notorious court cases during Pedro's reign was
the prosecution of two Roman Catholic bishops who
tried to put ecclesiastical decrees above civil law.   They
were condemned to prison and hard labor.

The largest part of the emperor's day was devoted
to keeping in close touch with the life and activities of
his people, and visiting public institutions.   He arose

promptly at six o'clock, read quantities of newspapers so that he knew what was happening all over the world; attended to business matters until half-past nine, his breakfast hour; then met those who had appointments with him; later he inspected the National Library, the Military Academy, the government machine shops, or hospitals and public schools. After dinner he would work in his library or laboratory, attend the theater, of which he was very fond, or some state function. When, in 1850, a terrible epidemic of cholera broke out, attacking an average of two hundred people a day, Dom Pedro constantly visited the hospitals, sat by patients, gave lavishly of his help and encouragement, and even acted as nurse on many occasions.

The emperor always said that one of the most delightful days he ever spent was on the American merchant-steamer *City of Pittsburg,* which had anchored in the harbor of Rio to take on coal. The captain had planned an all-day "picnic" and excursion down the coast for Dom Pedro, his family, Cabinet, and important officials. The party, all in full court dress except the emperor and empress, arrived in state barges. United States and Brazilian flags waved from every mast of the ship and a full orchestra played the national anthems of the two countries. As she steamed out through the harbor, Brazilian men-of-war saluted with cannon, and the Imperial navy down to the last sailor shouted vivas. Dom Pedro meanwhile lost no time about investigating the inner workings of the steamer, which for those days was a magnificent specimen of naval architecture. He clambered down narrow, oily ladders, and squeezed through minute passageways in the midst of the machinery to the very hottest and lowest corners of the ship, inspecting everything from the engine to the coal-bunkers.

An enterprising American who arranged an exhibit of United States industries, held in the national museum of Rio, tells how he conducted the Emperor about the hall as his particular guest of honor. "His Majesty commenced at one end, and with great earnestness and interest examined everything in detail. He made many inquiries, and manifested a most intimate knowledge of the progress of our country." At the table displaying beautiful bound books sent by New York publishers, the emperor "opened the *Homes of the American Authors,* and surprised me by his knowledge of our literature. He made remarks on Irving, Cooper, and Prescott, showing an intimate acquaintance with each. His eye falling on the name of Longfellow, he asked me, with great haste and eagerness, *'Avez-vous les poèmes de Monsieur Longfellow?'* It was the first time that I ever saw Dom Pedro II. manifest an enthusiasm which in its earnestness and simplicity resembled the warmth of childhood when about to possess itself of some long cherished object." As the two men parted, Dom Pedro said: "When you return to your country, have the kindness to say to Mr. Longfellow how much pleasure he has given me."

In 1863 several Brazilian vessels were captured by the English, diplomatic relations between the empire and Great Britain were broken off, and the people became dangerously excited. For all his quiet tastes there was an iron streak in Dom Pedro which commanded and held the confidence of his subjects in time of emergency. At this crisis he quieted them with the simple dignity of his words: "I am above all a Brazilian and as such more than any one interested in maintaining intact the dignity and honor of the nation. As I confide in my people, the people should confide in me and my government which will proceed as circumstances shall demand, in such a manner that the title 'Brazilians' of which we are proud will suffer no outrage. Where the honor and sovereignty of the nation fall, there will I fall with it." War was averted, but the episode woke the nation to a realizing sense of its maritime weakness. By a large donation from his own salary Dom Pedro gave impetus to a nationwide preparedness campaign and funds were speedily raised for the purchase of ironclads and ammunition.

Two years later fifty-seven battalions of volunteers responded to the emperor's call to arms. Paraguay and her tyrant dictator had declared war, and Brazil, in the midst of her years of peace and prosperity, was called upon to show her military prowess. It was the only long and costly war of Pedro's reign, and by it Brazil won her right to free navigation on the Paraguay River. The Brazilians to-day are proud of the records made then by their soldiers and sailors.

"The history of no other war," it has been said, "contains more examples of heroic and hopeless charges, or stories of more desperate hand-to-hand fighting." When the war was over Dom Pedro made a voluntary pledge to protect for ten years the independence of the little country he had just defeated, until it could recover its strength and look out for itself. It meant "Hands off" for all the other Republics.

Every time he left his country to travel abroad Dom Pedro added great prestige to Brazil, and when he came home he brought with him all the progressive ideas of other lands. In Europe he visited schools, museums, charitable institutions, industrial plants, and observatories, as energetically as the casual tourist visits ancient ruins. Many honors were given him by historical and scientific societies. The gayest city in the world made a social lion of this staid scholar and bookworm. "The man really in fashion in the metropolis of the French Republic," says one writer, "was the emperor. He lived in the Grand Hotel, admitted visitors, and talked to all intelligently and modestly. In general he reserved to himself the right to ask questions. He attended balls, frequented scientific institutions, and lost no opportunity of gaining knowledge. He saw all the notable pictures, he went to the conservatory, the race-course, the exchange, and the opera." Every phase of life interested him.

All official honors, hospitality and court functions planned for him simply because he was an emperor, Dom Pedro politely declined. The first experience he had on his trip to Europe proved the sincerity of his desire to lay aside royal prerogatives while he took his holiday. When his steamer reached Lisbon all the passengers had to be quarantined. "The king of Portugal, a nephew of the emperor, wished to make an exception of Dom Pedro," so the story is told, "and sent a special steamer fitted up in royal style commanded by officers of the navy to convey His Royal Majesty to the shore where his royal nephew and a palace awaited him and his empress. The emperor asked if his fellow passengers were also to be exempted from quarantine. Receiving a negative reply he immediately said: 'Thank His Majesty Dom Luis, and say to him, that I am traveling incognito; hence I am subject to the same laws as these gentlemen who came with me on the *Douro* and I will serve out the quarantine with them.'" The emperor remained with the rest in the uncomfortable quarantine building.

Dom Pedro was the first monarch who ever visited the United States. On the occasion of the great Centennial Exposition in Philadelphia in 1876 he saw a wonderful opportunity for his country, and he decided to go, as a plain citizen of Brazil, "to be present at the celebration of the close of a century of freedom in a great constitutional country, and to aid in representing the products and industries of the second nation on the American continent." At the grand opening of the Exposition, President Grant and His Majesty Dom Pedro went together on a trip of inspection through the vast buildings and both touched the little lever that started the motive power for all the machines on exhibition. The Brazilian department was a great success, winning three and one half times as many premiums as any other South American country. The emperor and the exhibits combined opened the eyes of thousands of American business men to the tremendous natural resources and industrial possibilities of the empire.

For three months Dom Pedro traveled through the United States, devoting an average of sixteen hours a day to sightseeing and investigation. When he had finished he pronounced Boston his favorite city. He particularly enjoyed visiting Lowell, Longfellow and Whittier, whose works he knew almost by heart. Some of them he had translated into Portuguese. Longfellow once said that his "Story of King Robert of Sicily" had been translated into Portuguese by three poets, but that by the emperor was the best of all. Many prominent Americans entertained Dom Pedro in their homes, and scientific, historical and geographical societies held special meetings in his honor. The New York Historical Society elected him an honorary member and the highest tributes were paid him. "Dom Pedro II," said a speaker of the evening, "by his character, his taste, his application and acquisitions in literature and science ascends from the mere fortuitous position as emperor and takes his place in the world as a *man*."

In New York, Dom Pedro often arose at six o'clock while his staff was still sleeping, and did some sightseeing before breakfast. On his very first day in the city, a Sunday, instead of resting after his 5,000-mile journey from Rio, he began at once on his program of "going everywhere, observing everything and questioning everybody." He went first to early mass at the Cathedral. Then he spent an hour at one of the famous services which Dwight L. Moody and Ira D. Sankey were holding in the old Hippodrome. During the rest of the day he visited a newsboys' home, the headquarters of the city fire department, and several police stations. There was very little of New York that he had not investigated before he left. "Well," said some one afterwards, "he certainly would have made a first-class reporter if he hadn't been a king."

The greatest national event during Dom Pedro's reign was the abolition of slavery, and no one worked harder to bring it to pass than the emperor himself. The African slave-trade had been abolished in 1850 and from that time on public opinion grew more and more in favor of emancipation, in spite of the strong opposition of planters and wealthy slave owners. Following Dom Pedro's example many high-minded citizens freed their own slaves. The slave was enabled to free himself in many ways, such as raising his own purchase money. The incentive to do this was great, for an ambitious slave had plenty of chance to rise in the world. "Some of the most intelligent men I met with in Brazil," says one writer, "were of African descent. If a man has freedom, money and merit, no matter how black his skin may be, no place in society is refused him. In the colleges, the medical, law and theological schools, there is no distinction of color." Plots of ground were frequently given to the freedmen for cultivation, and the government encouraged them to become independent planters.

After many hot debates the General Assembly passed a law in 1871 declaring free from that date all children of slave mothers, and all the government slaves. In the next fifteen years the number of slaves decreased by one half. Dom Pedro's dearest wish was that he might live to see every slave in the country a free man, and this wish came true in the last year of his reign. He had gone abroad in poor health, leaving his daughter Isabel as regent. When Congress met, the Princess railroaded the abolition law through both Houses in eight days and signed the bill which put the law into immediate force. It was the last act of the royal dynasty of Brazil.

In 1889 a Republican revolt took the whole empire by surprise. It had long been brewing beneath the surface, but so great was the emperor's popularity that Republicans had tactitly agreed to postpone the new government until his death. A rumor that Dom Pedro might abdicate in favor of Princess Isabel and thus initiate another generation of monarchy precipitated the revolution. The Republican leagues, with the backing of the army and navy, refused to wait any longer. Dom Pedro, summoned from Petropolis by telegram, found a provisional government already organized when he reached the capital. In the Imperial Palace at Rio, surrounded by insurgents, the old emperor was told briefly that his long reign was over.

"We are forced to notify you," said the ultimatum, "that the provisional government expects from your patriotism the sacrifice of leaving Brazilian territory with your family in the shortest possible time."

Dom Pedro II. replied simply: "I resolve to submit to the command of circumstances and will depart with my family for Europe to-morrow, leaving this beloved country to which I have tried to give firm testimony of my love and my dedication during nearly half a century as chief of the State. I shall always have kind remembrances of Brazil and hopes for its prosperity." The next day the imperial family sailed for Lisbon.

The Imperial coat of arms and flag were ordered to be torn down from all buildings; streets called after the royal family were renamed; the Dom Pedro Railway became the Central Railway of Brazil; and Pedro II. College was changed to National Institution of Instruction. In three days' time a monarchy had been overthrown without bloodshed or opposition. The emperor, who had sometimes been called the best Republican in Brazil, was replaced by a military dictator, and from that time to this the nation has known her share of civil war.

The homesick emperor, living in European hotels or rented villas, till the time of his death in 1891, "always remained as one on the point of departure, as if he ever expected to be recalled by his former subjects, a hope which till the last moment would not die out of his heart." To the "last American monarch" an American pays this tribute in the dedication of his book on South America :[1]

TO
H. M. DOM PEDRO II.
EMPEROR OF BRAZIL
SCHOLAR AND SCIENTIST, PATRON OF
ARTS AND LETTERS,
STERLING STATESMAN AND MODEL MONARCH,
WHOSE REIGN OF HALF A CENTURY HAS BEEN
ZEALOUSLY AND SUCCESSFULLY DEVOTED TO
PUBLIC INSTRUCTION, INDUSTRIAL
ENTERPRISE, AND THE ABOLITION
OF SLAVERY
THROUGHOUT THE VAST AND OPULENT
"EMPIRE OF THE SOUTHERN CROSS"

[1]Vincent, *Around and About South America.*

DAVID TRUMBULL

DAVID TRUMBULL

DAVID TRUMBULL

A long, narrow strip of crowded, bustling wharves and business streets, a steep rise of two hundred feet to quiet green hills topped with gay gardens and pretty villas washed in white or blue, snow-crowned Mount Aconcagua in the background, and down in front the blue bay full of ships from all over the world —this is the Valparaiso of to-day, chief port on the western coast of South America. But when David Trumbull, from New England, stood at the railing of the *Mississippi* as she sailed into the harbor on Christmas day in 1845, "there was not a tree in sight save a cactus on a hilltop. The houses were so scattered as to make little impression, and one would say, 'Where *is* the city?'"

On every side were sailing vessels. All the ships from New England and the eastern coast of the Americas on their long journey around Cape Horn up to the northwest coast after whales and seals, or to California a few years later when gold was discovered, put in at Valparaiso for supplies and repairs. The old town was a port of call for all merchant and fishing vessels plying along the coast. In the course of one year 1,500 of them anchored in the bay, representing nearly thirty different nations, and 15,000 sailors ran wild in town. To reach this rough, ever-changing population, much of it British and American, David Trumbull had volunteered to go to Valparaiso. His was the first sailor mission in South America.

Trumbull belonged to a fine old New England family, staunch Congregationalists, descendants of John Alden and "the Puritan maiden, Priscilla," and later of old Jonathan Trumbull, governor of Connecticut when Washington was president of the United States. One of this famous family, Henry Clay Trumbull, once said: "The question is, not whether you are proud of your grandfather, but whether your grandfather would be proud of you. It is a good thing to be in a family line which had a fine start long ago, and has been and still is improving generation by generation. It is a sad thing to be in a family line where the best men and women were in former generations." David was always proud of his ancestors. He once "danced like a schoolboy" when he found proof that the only one ever charged with illiteracy had written his own will. His ancestors would have been equally proud of him, for his is one of the greatest names in the Trumbull family.

After his school days were over, he had a taste of business life in New York—his only "commercial experience," he called it. But it was the wrong trail for David and he quickly changed his mind. He prepared for Yale, and entered in the fall of 1838, just before his nineteenth birthday, bent on being a minister. In the intimacy of school and university life men are quick to discover the caliber of their companions. Trumbull passed muster with high honors, and his status in the college community was an enviable one. "In all that he said or did," said a Yale friend, "there was displayed a certain nobility of character which was the more attractive as it seemed so natural to him. He had a rich vein of humor; and we will add—as it seems to have been a characteristic that was often made a subject of remark during all his life—his face wore a peculiarly joyous expression, which was quite remarkable, and gave an additional charm to the genial smile with which he always greeted those to whom he spoke."

The very year that he graduated from Princeton Theological Seminary, he heard that the Foreign Evangelical Society wanted a young minister to go to Chile. It was a splendid opening for a man of big mentality equal to grappling with difficult situations. There were no Protestant missions, no Protestant churches on the whole west coast. Pioneer work was what Trumbull wanted. It would be like owning his own business—he could build it up just as he pleased. Out of nothing at all he could create something of great and lasting value. Before he left the family home at Colchester, Connecticut, for Chile, he took his pen and wrote down definitely, so that "he might be able to keep it more in mind," what he considered to be the agreement with God which he had made. In it he said among other things: "My God, I will begin a new life. . . . I will aim to please thee every day forward. . . . In my public life as a minister, I will study thy word, and all truth where it can be found, in candor, with prayer; and will apply myself to find out suitable languages, figures and thoughts, that others may be taught by my efforts. . . . Accept me then with all my powers, not as a gift, but as a *favor to myself*. Fit me to serve thee, and then make use of me. Do just thy pleasure." Then he signed his name to the prayer as to a contract.

Trumbull preached his first sermon to the sailors on board the *Mississippi,* anchored in Valparaiso Bay, a few days after his arrival; his first sermon on shore at a little printing shop, with a "printer's horse" for a pulpit and rolls of paper for pews. His first friend in the strange, ugly little city was the chaplain of a small Episcopalian congregation which met in a private room for services on Sunday.

Public worship was forbidden. A Protestant in South America was as much lost as a man without a country. He had no church, no social position, no legal rights. Civil marriage was not allowed, and it was almost impossible for him to find a way to be married, except on board an English or American ship outside the three-mile area of sea over which a country has control. All the cemeteries were owned by the Catholic Church, and the only burial place for a Protestant in Valparaiso was the dumping ground outside the city. Many well-to-do residents, English, Scotch, American or German business men, once Protestant, had drifted into the Roman Church, simply because there had been nothing else to do, or because their friends or the Chilean women they married were Catholics. "Some of the most potential Roman Catholics here today," Trumbull wrote home, "are of British origin; their parents or grandparents, having had no public worship to attract them, have attended none, and their wives, worthy and good Catholics, have carried their children into that connection, unless they have gone into free thinking."

To conserve this drifting population he organized a Union Church in 1847, with fifteen charter members. All those who had no church of their own he welcomed into his. At first a warehouse was rented for the services, but it was small and so dark that whale-oil lamps had to be lighted even in broad daylight. For seven years the church had no home of its own. Then enough money was saved to buy a plot of land and put up a little building—the first Protestant church in South America. It was hard work even to finish making it. City officials ordered Trumbull to give up his absurd plans, and threatened to call out the police. A Protestant church would be an outrage to the community, and a service held publicly would be breaking the law. Good Catholics were horrified and the priests prepared for battle.

But Trumbull was a capable fighter himself, and he had substantial backing in a number of English and Scotch merchants, influential residents, who belonged to his church. For six months matters were at a standstill. Then the government compromised. Services might be held on these conditions: that the building be entirely surrounded by a high wooden fence with one small, inconspicuous gate, shutting off any view from the street; and that hymns and anthems be sung so softly that passersby could never hear them and be tempted to step in to listen. Now at last the Protestant had his niche in the community, and David Trumbull's great ambition was to widen it until Protestant and Catholic should have equal rights and one church no longer control the affairs of state. The vision of the young minister who had come to preach to the sailors of one port had widened until it took in a whole country, a changed constitution, the overthrow of century-old tradition. "The symbols of religion remain," he wrote of Latin America, "but religion itself has gone. The shadow remains, but the substance has fled." And so, sailors, foreign residents, Chilean people—Trumbull set himself to reach them all, to give them a bit of the genuine spirit of Christ which is the foundation for thought and conduct among all the great nations of earth.

His work among the seamen was the entering wedge. On the ships, in the city hospital where there were always sick sailors, in the jails where other unhappy specimens spent most of their time ashore, Trumbull searched them out, and not a sailor but felt that he had at least one friend in the city. Officials who at first had wanted nothing better than to find fault with him, began to appreciate the neighborliness and good will of the young minister, and gave him permission to go ahead and do anything he liked so long as he worked only among the crews of vessels anchored in the harbor, and among non-Spanish-speaking people. So down on the waterfront he opened a Bethel, headquarters for his mission, with flag flying over it so that no sailor could miss seeing it when he passed by.

In 1850 he married a girl from his own New England State, and with her help started a school for girls, "for the education of those who were to be the mothers of the next generation of Chileans." All schools were Catholic then, and the authorities looked with suspicion upon this upstart school in their midst. They hastened to send an examining committee to pick flaws in it, but the committee found nothing it could honestly condemn and came away with high recommendation for the whole enterprise.

Editing newspapers and publishing pamphlets were two of Trumbull's favorite diversions. He wanted to discuss the big questions of the day before the widest possible audience, and, like Sarmiento, hammer daily on the public conscience until ideas of progress and reform were firmly lodged in people's minds. He published and edited the first Protestant paper in Spanish, calling it *La Piedra,* which means "The Rock." On the title page were those words of Christ to Peter: "Thou art Peter, and upon this rock I will build my church." It came out as often as he could gather enough funds to print it. He also published *The Record* in English, *El Heraldo,* a Santiago newspaper, and wrote sermons and editorials for a number of Spanish dailies. One time a letter came to him from a society of workingmen, which he sent home to show his friends because it pleased him so much:

"We make it our duty to give you our best thanks in the name of the society. Our statutes do not allow the discussion of religion or politics while in session, but afterwards, adjourning, your periodical is read and each offers his remarks upon it. . . . Progress and knowledge are advancing rapidly and are waking up minds that have been asleep. Sons of the common people, we from our youth have been educated in the practises of Romanism, and they who know the truth pure and spotless are very few; hence it is necessary that those apostles who try to make it known should be unfaltering in the use of the press in bringing out their publications."

Whenever Trumbull found something he wanted the people to read he had it translated and printed first, and collected the money to pay for it second. He was so often in process of securing funds for one and another good cause, and so successful in doing it, that he said his epitaph ought to be: "Here lies a good beggar."

He began a campaign for circulating Bibles, which, since the days of James Thomson, had gradually disappeared from the land under ban of the church. The archbishop published a letter declaring the Bible to be fraudulent and heretical, and forbidding its use. Trumbull then rode into the lists armed to the teeth with repartee. He answered the letter and kept on

answering letters till his opponent "withdrew in confusion." He liked a chance for a good newspaper
skirmish, because of the wide publicity it always gave
to his ideas, but "he was always the gentleman and
always the friend, and his polemics were full, not of
hard hitting only, but also of his genial kindness and
irresistible love." This was the secret of his success.
He knew how to get along with people.

The most celebrated skirmish of those years was a
series of public debates between Trumbull and a fiery
Catholic named Mariano Casanova. Dr. Robert E.
Speer tells the story: "In Chile there is a Saint of
Agriculture who guards the fortune of farmers, giving
them rich harvests and sending rain at the appointed
times. Since the seasons are fairly regular the good
offices of San Isidro are seldom required. Occasion-
ally, however, the rains are delayed, much to the loss
of the sower and the distress of the eater. At such
times mild measures are used to begin with, and the
saint is reminded of his duty by processions and prayers and placated by offerings. If he still refuses to
listen, his statue is banished from the church, even
manacled and beaten through the streets. In 1863
San Isidro answered the prayers of his devotees with
commendable promptitude. Eighteen hours after sup-
plications had been made at his altar rain fell in copi-
ous showers. In view of this signal blessing the archbishop called upon the faithful for contributions to
repair San Isidro's shabby church. It was at this junc-
ture that Dr. Trumbull entered the lists, and in an arti-

cle entitled "Who Gives the Rain?" he attacked the practise of saint worship. Casanova replied and the battle was on. Charge and countercharge followed in rapid succession. The affair got into the provincial papers and was discussed all over the country. San Isidro and rain became the question of the day; and at last Casanova withdrew from the field, routed foot and horse."

In all enterprises which were for the public welfare Dr. Trumbull coöperated heartily with the Roman Catholics, adapting himself just so far as he could to the life of the community. Once when a bishop wanted to publish an inexpensive edition of a Catholic New Testament, Dr. Trumbull helped him collect funds, some of which came from members of Union Church. One year a terrible cholera plague raged in the city. Dr. Trumbull was appointed a member of the relief committee and joined forces with the Catholics in relieving the distress of the poor and providing extra hospital space. Again he set to work to collect money, sending a substantial sum to the *curé* of San Felipe, who afterward wrote him: "That God, who has promised to reward the cup of cold water given in his name, may crown you with all good, is my desire."

In all communities there are men who have a hand in every good work, whose names appear on committees and governing boards, whose influence is felt in matters of state, of commerce, of education. Trumbull was such a man, a leader of national reform, the friend and adviser of the Liberal party. He had once been looked upon with suspicion and hatred. As the years passed by he gained such recognition and respect in Valparaiso and other parts of Chile that "a prestige began to surround him." His dream of reaching the Chilean people as well as the foreign population began to come true. With the backing of the Liberal party he made the first feeble little step toward religious liberty by pushing a bill through Congress which permitted "dissenters" to worship in private, and to establish private schools for their children. But they were not allowed to build any church which looked like a church. It must be elaborately disguised. There must be no telltale bell or steeple to distinguish it from any private house or hall. Before this the services in Union Church had been allowed as a favor to influential British merchants. Now they became strictly legal. Ten years later he could write: "The elections for Congress and president are approaching; in the platforms of the parties it is encouraging to notice that religious freedom occupies a prominent place."

The cemetery bill and the civil marriage act were the two reforms upon which Dr. Trumbull had set his heart, not only for the sake of foreigners but for the great masses of Chileans who were too poor to pay the exorbitant fees demanded by the priests for burial and marriage rites. The marriage ceremony had become such a luxury that a great percentage of the people decided they could get along very well without it, and the moral fiber of the state grew steadily weaker. After eight years of fighting, the cemetery

bill, allowing free burial, was passed by Congress in
1883, and four months later Dr. Trumbull reported:
"Our Congress has just passed a civil marriage bill
which deprives the Roman Catholic Church of all
superiority over other denominations and must reduce
its emoluments immensely."

Meanwhile Union Church grew influential and
wealthy enough to support its own ministry, so that
when the Presbyterian Board of Foreign Missions took
charge of the mission work in Chile, it found an independent congregation, which, far from needing help,
stood ready to give both money and coöperation to the
Presbyterian mission. Dr. Trumbull longed to have the
Board extend its mission work to other cities. "As
yet this whole line of coast seems to be left out of
everybody's calculations," he wrote. "Its inhabitants
would be better off if they lived in Asia. Is America
so poor a name to divine by? . . . Why are these less
important to care for than people in the center of
Africa, so that when Stanley tells of them half a dozen
missionary societies rush to occupy the ground, and
here not a single one?" Another letter says: "The
manager of the steamship company told me only yesterday that they have five hundred men, English, in
Callao, but that there is no service. I know from a
number of these men that they desire to have worship;
their decided preference is Presbyterian, and you are
the people that ought to give it to them. If you will
provide it, you will win credit and you will have
assistance. Only do not wait for anybody to ask it,

nor for anybody to promise anything. Just sail in like
Farragut into Mobile Bay; consider yourself that
gallant and daring admiral up in the maintop of the
Richmond, tied by your waist so as not to fall, and
capture the forts of Callao harbor."

The Trumbull home in Valparaiso, built high on
the cliffs overlooking the city, was a delightful place
to visit. Dr. John Trumbull, one of the sons, says:
"With all that my father did, he ever found time to
be with and help his children. After my father married Jane Wales Fitch, they came out to Chile on an
independent basis, supporting themselves by conducting a young ladies' school for eight or ten years; then,
at the request of Union Church, he consented to give
it up and devote himself entirely to pastoral and church
work, though they were only able to offer as a salary
half of what he was then making. At that time I can
remember that we had to give up horseback riding—
for my brother David and I had been in the habit of
riding out to Fisherman's Bay every morning with
father for a dip and a swim—in fact, I was but five
when he taught us to swim and even to jump off of
the spring-board into deep water—and take to footing
it. He believed in all manly sports, which, according
to him, included everything but shooting, of which he
never approved; and he taught or encouraged us to
walk, run, play cricket, ride, climb, swim, dive, row,
fish, cook, and so forth. On holidays we often went
off as a family on picnics to the country, or up the
hills and ravines back of Valparaiso, and were taught,

like the Boy Scouts of the present day, to be self-reliant and ready for any and every emergency.

"Winter evenings he was in the habit of reading aloud to us Goldsmith's *Vicar of Wakefield,* Bunyan's *Pilgrim's Progress,* Dickens' *Nicholas Nickleby,* Scott's *Old Mortality,* and Irving's *Knickerbocker Stories* and *Life of Washington.*

"People might wonder how he found time for all he did. The secret of it was that he was ever an early riser. By five we were off on our rides or walks, and before that he had often got in an hour's work; and during his later years he had by eight o'clock already done a good day's work.

"As to his children, it was often said the Trumbull children never had any bringing up—that, like Topsy, they simply 'growed.' Certainly I can remember but two trouncings—one for playing with matches at bonfires on the shingle roof of our house, which, as firemen, we had to extinguish; and again for playing with my brother at William Tell, using a potato which we alternately balanced on our heads, and an old-fashioned musket on which we used up half a box of caps.

"To show that my father's discipline was guided by a tactful wisdom it might be worth while to record that when, as a boy just fifteen years of age, I was sent off alone to the United States, the only sermon which I got was the following: 'John, my boy, there is only one fear that I have in your going from home; and that is, that, since you are so good-natured and ready to please, you may not have the manliness to say no.' That remark drove home, as you can well understand, for once a boy realizes the cowardice of yielding to temptation, the battle against it is more than half won, and I am free to acknowledge that that did more to stiffen my moral backbone than any other spoken word I ever heard.

"We were a large family—four boys and three girls who lived to grow up. All of the boys were sent to Yale and studied professions, while the girls went either to Wellesley or Smith, and were sent, too, by a pastor who had no private means. Good business instincts he had, and that helped; but what really enabled him to give his children an education was that he and my mother were willing to take in young Englishmen as boarders, giving them a home and at the same time receiving payment, so as to let their children have an education. On that he laid great stress, saying that all his desire was to give us an education and let us 'shift without a penny.'"

While Dr. Trumbull was working so hard for the people of Chile, three of his big, merry family died within a short time of each other and just at the age when they were beginning to be of greatest use in the world. The oldest son, David, a student in Yale School of Theology, dived from a yacht off the coast of New London, in an effort to save a boy's life. There was no tender or small boat with the yacht, and by the time his friends were able to tack and reach him he sank. The boy, whom he held up with his last ounce of strength, was saved. Mary Trumbull died a few months after graduating from Wellesley, and Stephen, a physician, died of yellow fever at sea, on the way to Valparaiso.

As Dr. Trumbull grew old among the people he had learned to think of almost as his own countrymen, he decided to adopt the country where he had lived and worked for forty years. One day he appeared before the proper authorities and asked for the privilege of taking out naturalization papers. The usual legal proceedings were waived in his case and the president and all his Chilean friends rejoiced in this proof of his love for Chile. There was no doubt of his welcome. One friend said: "Valparaiso has before felt honored in claiming him as the most worthy and best known of her foreign residents. Now we regard him as a fellow countryman and a true brother." When some of his American friends wrote how surprised and disturbed they were that he had renounced his American citizenship he confessed his reason for doing it. There had been times, during the long years when he was fighting for reforms, that everything seemed utterly hopeless. Then he had made another vow to God. If ever his wishes were realized and the reforms became law, he would express his gratitude by becoming a citizen of Chile. He had kept his vow.

But a descendant of the Aldens must always have loved America best. One of Dr. Trumbull's friends says: "Surrounded by foreigners, he defended his country as bravely as his Continental ancestors did before him. No Britisher, even in friendly jest, could

speak slightingly of the States and escape unwounded.
Once an Englishman at his table remarked, 'I never
could understand, Doctor, how you keep that picture
on your wall, and in such a conspicuous place, too.'
The picture represented the *Essex* in Valparaiso Bay,
striking her colors to two English men-of-war. With
a smile, and in his dulcet voice, the host replied: 'I
wouldn't take anything for that picture.   It's the greatest curiosity in the house; for it is the only instance in
history where an American vessel ever hauled down
her flag to an enemy.   Can you duplicate that in English history?' "

On a great stone in the cemetery of Valparaiso is
one of countless tributes from his best friends, the people of Chile:

MEMORIAE SACRUM
The Reverend
David Trumbull, D.D.
Founder and Minister of the Union Church, Valparaiso
Born in Elizabeth, N. J., 1st of Nov., 1819
Died in Valparaiso, 1st of Feb., 1889

For forty-three years he gave himself to unwearied and
successful effort
In the cause of evangelical truth and religious liberty in
this country.
As a gifted and faithful minister, and as a friend he
was honored and
Loved by foreign residents on this coast.   In his public
life he was the
Counselor of statesmen, the supporter of every good
enterprise, the
Helper of the poor, and the consoler of the afflicted.

In memory of
His eminent services, fidelity, charity and sympathy
this monument
Has been raised by his friends in this community
And by citizens of his adopted country.

One of Dr. Trumbull's Yale friends, writing an "In Memoriam," says: "Perhaps never among any Spanish-speaking people, in either hemisphere, has an Anglo-Saxon, or a Protestant, received such a testimonial of the popular respect. . . . What Livingstone did for Africa was done for South America by David Trumbull."

FRANCISCO PENZOTTI

FRANCISCO PENZOTTI

(Imprisoned in Callao, Peru)

FRANCISCO PENZOTTI

"Never in my life have I fought so much with priests and friars as in these last months . . . there hardly passes a night when I do not dream of being in combat with them." These, his own words, tell a common experience of Señor Francisco Penzotti's life in South America as distributing agent of the American Bible Society. The business of such an agent is to sell Bibles to all who will buy them, and like all evangelical work it has been carried on in the face of the most desperate opposition on the part of the Roman Catholic clergy, who control the religious life of the State. One of the beliefs of the Roman Church is that the Bible, as we know it, should not be placed in the hands of the ignorant because they will misinterpret its teachings. The only version allowed for common use is the result of careful pruning and editing by the papal hierarchy, believed to be the only infallible authority.

And so, when the agents for the Bible Society opened Bible shops, and canvassed city and town from door to door, peddling the best book in the world, not in English—that would not have bothered the priests—but in Spanish, the people's own language, the alarmed bishops rose up in their pulpits and urged that all unite in their efforts to crush "these monsters of heresy."

Ignorant, fanatical, warped in spirit and morals, the majority of clergy in South America have done little credit to their Church, and it is with this powerful priest ring, never truly representative of the Catholic faith at its best, that progressive elements have continually been at war. The dramatic experiences of Señor Penzotti first held up for ridicule before the eyes of the whole world the absurd spectacle of fourteenth century bigotry lingering on at the end of the nineteenth.

Penzotti was born in Italy in 1851, of staunch Roman Catholic parents. When thirteen years old he was invited by relatives to go with them to South America. It seemed to his boyish imagination like a fairyland of promise, and he set off with the same high hopes that bring the ambitious immigrant to New York. For many years he lived in Montevideo, capital of Uruguay, passively accepting the only religious faith he knew anything about. Then one night—he was now twenty-five years old—a friend proposed in an idle moment that, just for the novelty of it, they drop in at a theater where a preaching service was to be held.

"I went with him more from curiosity than interest," Penzotti said afterward. "We entered what had been a theater, and what was then the only place of preaching the gospel in the city. Later the house became known as the Thirty-third Street Temple of the Methodist Episcopal Church. . . . I went out from there that night profoundly impressed." No

Protestant in the city was half so energetic during the next few weeks in attending services as Penzotti. His enthusiasm and his talents attracted attention and he was appointed an evangelist of the little embryo church which was struggling so hard to make a place for itself in the community. "Naturally I did not have the experience at that time which I now possess," he says, "but instead I should like to possess to-day the zeal and energy of those times."

Arrangements to launch the work of Bible distribution in the northern republics, particularly Bolivia, had just been completed. Penzotti was chosen to accompany Mr. Andrew Milne, the agent, on a preliminary trip through these new and difficult regions. The last man who had dared to sell Bibles in Bolivia had been murdered and thrown into the river, and the exploring party received due warning of what they might expect: "Huge mountains bar the way to the circulation of God's word there; mountains of prejudice and obstacles, that are only equaled by the immense Andes themselves for altitude and difficulty, have to be scaled and overcome." They met with unexpected success, however. The civil authorities helped them; the people, when not too much afraid of the priests, were eager to hear the preaching and read the Book; and in a few months over 5,000 Bibles were sold.

The next year Penzotti was put in charge of the campaign. Traveling in Bolivia in those days meant riding on mule-back over abominable roads or no roads

at all.   There were no inns; no hospitable friends
waiting to welcome him; often nothing but the bare
ground to sleep on after a hard day; and no extra
money for comforts of any kind.   But there were no
monotonous moments in that adventurous trip of
Penzotti's.   The unexpected always lay in wait around
the next corner.   In one of his audiences he was surprised to see a number of priests who listened with
courteous attention to all he had to say.   After the
service they hastened forward to shake hands and congratulate him on his eloquence.   They had come to
propose that he return to the Catholic fold, and as a
special inducement they promised that he should be
an ordained priest in a year's time.   In the next city
he was given the municipal hall for his meetings and
people crowded to hear him.   When the priest heard
of this he sent all the boys he could muster, armed with
rockets and tin horns, to interrupt the meeting, and for
a few minutes it was a hand-to-hand fight until the
rowdies were driven away.

The worst hornet's nest of all was the city of Cochabamba.   At first Penzotti made good sales, but as
soon as the priests discovered what was going on,
trouble began.   The bishop, whose slightest word carried great weight, circulated a warning among the
people against this "mutilated, adulterated and false"
Bible.   Penzotti managed such situations with a high
hand.   He took his Bible and a copy of the warning
and proceeded to the bishop's house.   He always liked
to have it out face to face with the priests.   "As he

did not know me, he gave me an entrance into his study," Penzotti tells the story. "Once there I told him that I was the one who had introduced the Bible which he was calling false. I put one of my Bibles in his hand and said to him: 'Be so kind as to prove what you have said, since, if you do not, I have the right to accuse you of libel before competent authorities.' It seemed to me that he was more frightened than I should have been able to be. If he had been another kind of man he would have had the people after me, and there would not have remained any more than my ashes!" But the bishop carelessly flipped over the pages and remarked profoundly that these might be the very best of books, yet since they were not approved by the Church he had a papal order not to admit them.

By this time the harm was done and the whole city grew threatening. Five hundred women belonging to a sacred order hurried from house to house to warn families not to buy Bibles under pain of excommunication. Priests trailed Penzotti wherever he went, crying: "Here comes the heretic! Beware!" A bonfire in a public square meant that his wares were being disposed of in the priests' own favorite fashion. "I went on with my work as before," he writes, "going from door to door, but in vain; there was not a living soul that did not know, and the sale stopped entirely. Indeed I had much to do to resist the return of the books already sold, and had it not been for the protection of the authorities I don't know how it might have fared with me. Several warned me that I ought to withdraw, as my life was in danger."

Penzotti always has a ready answer for priestly sallies. Once when he caught a priest in the act of twisting the meaning of a Bible verse, he publicly exposed the fraud. "Let me tell you that though you have the best of me this time," said the priest furiously, "this same Book says that the gates of hell shall not prevail."

"Much less the gates of the Vatican," returned Penzotti.

During his travels Penzotti found that the terrible poverty of the people was often a hindrance to the sales. Sometimes a fifty-cent Bible would be paid for in several installments. He frequently distributed books on approval. One old lady who had the rare opportunity of comparing her Romish Bible with the priest's own Bible, was greatly astonished to find the latter just like the Bible the dreadful stranger had left at her door. When she came upon the second commandment, she exclaimed: "To think that this should be here and the *padre* not teach it to us! He must be deceiving us in other things, too; I shall learn for myself." She kept her new Bible.

"After I left Cochabamba," Penzotti reported, "several persons rushed into print, each one giving my ears a pull, but withal I have no doubt it will in the end contribute to the furtherance of the work." It did. As often happens, opposition makes fine advertising, and the fame of Penzotti and his book spread far and wide.

From Bolivia he crossed over into Chile, a difficult journey over the mountains. "You have to cross at a height of 18,000 feet," he wrote, "where there are no living beings nor vegetation of any kind. The only indication of the way is the line of white dry bones of beasts of burden and travelers killed in snow storms." In the Chilean towns he was well received and preached to large audiences who usually gathered in the town hall or a theater. From one town he reported: "Mr. Milne was here last year and sold so many Bibles that most people have them. As a result, there is a greater demand now for other instructive books of which we have only a limited supply." At the end of thirteen months of constant preaching, canvassing and traveling Penzotti returned to Montevideo. In all this time not a line from his family or friends had reached him because, as he said, "in the places where I visited and was persecuted, one of the forms which the persecution took was the capturing of my correspondence."

Penzotti tells the story of a little colony of enthusiastic Protestants which sprang up all by itself in one Chilean town: "A little more than a half century ago this place was destroyed by a tidal wave. When the waters retired the people went to remove the ruins in search of what they could find. One man found, below a strata of sand and mud, a book. For curiosity's sake he carried it to his house, where he cleaned it and put it out to dry.   It happened to be a New Testament.   It was a book unknown to him, so he read it to see what it was all about.   Various neighbors gathered to listen to the reading of the marvelous book, and when I visited this place I found the man at the head of an interesting group of people, all converted by that book dug out from the mud."

Because of his rare gifts as a Bible salesman, Penzotti was appointed agent for the Pacific coast by the American Bible Society in 1887, the year after his trip through the north.   "He is one to go forward where others turn back," it was said of him, "and he not only understands his work but loves it."   So they gave him the most important and difficult field of all, Peru.   With his family he went to Callao to live and there in the heart of the enemies' country he tackled the problem of religious freedom single-handed.

"Very little had been done with the Bible," he says, "and the gospel had never been preached in the language of the country.   My first care was hunting a place where I could preach to the people.   Then I went from door to door with the Bible, reading to the people, explaining it to them, and inviting them to attend the meetings.

"My first audience consisted of two people besides ourselves.   The following Sunday four people came; the next ten; then we went up to twenty; after that, to forty, fifty, sixty, eighty, until the hall could hold no more, and the problem of hunting a larger place presented itself.   It was with difficulty that we were able to find anything, and then what we found was in such poor condition that with our own hands we had to fix the ceiling, floor, lights, and make benches and other necessary furniture. Many of those who were interested came every night to get it ready. At the same time I had to raise funds for the rent and to buy materials."

From pulpit and press attacks came thick and fast, and the civil authorities, wishing to keep their popularity with the ruling class, did little to stop outbreaks of violence in the streets. One city official at least was not afraid to express his opinion. The clergy brought him a petition demanding the banishment of Señor Penzotti. He told them he would attend a meeting and see for himself what terrible harm there was in it. He liked it. When the priests called next day he said to them: "What do you wish to do to the gentleman anyway? He preaches the truth and that is precisely the thing we need."

Among other little tricks, the ingenious priests sold thin paper images of the Virgin for which they claimed miraculous powers. Whenever a foreigner carrying a valise came into sight, this figure must be rolled into a pill and swallowed as a means of protection against the impending evil! Processions formed and marched past Penzotti's house shouting: "Long live the Apostolic Roman Catholic religion!" and "Death to Penzotti! Down with the Protestants!" Showers of stones and mud were thrown at the house and insulting epithets were chalked on its walls. Crowds of men, and even women, would gather in front of the old warehouse used for the services, and lie in wait to molest any one who went in or out. The keyhole was so often stopped up with pebbles that a padlock finally had to be put on the inside of the door. One night a priest fastened on a padlock of his own and locked in the whole audience. Then he crossed to the sidewalk opposite to watch what happened.

"There was no other way of getting out than by that door," says Penzotti. "There were a number of windows but they were very high and had gratings. One of the brothers did not come to the meeting that night. About nine o'clock he felt a desire to come, but said to himself: 'It is very late; the meeting will be over now.' Yet it seemed that something told him to go to the hall; and so he just put on his hat and came. On reaching the door he heard us singing a hymn. He wanted to come in but the door was locked with a padlock on the outside. He could not imagine what had happened, and then the thought came: 'Some enemy has done this!' Feeling around in his pocket he discovered a key that unlocked the padlock. He opened the door. The priest who was observing on the opposite sidewalk, lifted his hands to his head exclaiming: 'These heretics have the devil's own protection!'"

Penzotti had been particularly warned to keep away from Arequipa, the most Catholic city in the whole country. Sure enough, he had been there only a few hours when his arrest was ordered by an influential bishop, he was clapped into jail on the charge of selling corrupt literature, and his boxes of books confiscated. During nineteen days of imprisonment Penzotti made friends among the other prisoners and held services for them. They seemed to like what they heard, especially the inspector who had arrested him at the mayor's command. When the order for his release came from the president at Lima, Penzotti found the beaming inspector waiting at the prison door to congratulate him and invite him home to breakfast.

A few months later, in July, 1890, Penzotti was arrested and imprisoned in Callao without bail. The article of the Peruvian constitution which he was accused before the court of crimes of violating was this: "The State professes and protects the Apostolic Roman Catholic religion, excluding all other public worship." As a matter of fact Penzotti had taken great pains beforehand to understand this law and act within his rights; for he had been told by the Peruvian minister of justice, through the United States legation: "You can do whatever the constitution allows and nothing that it forbids." A service of worship, to be considered "private," had to be held in an orderly manner, with closed doors, and no one admitted except by tickets obtained in advance. These requirements had been scrupulously met. For seventy years the Church of England in Peru had held services in English and met with no opposition; while on the same block with Penzotti's warehouse, the Chinese population peacefully worshiped in their joss house.

The whole situation was just this: the Roman Church would not tolerate Protestant preaching in the Spanish language.

"The plan of my enemies in placing me in an unbearable cell," said Penzotti, "was that I might die in it, or solicit liberty on condition that I leave the country. When I had been in prison forty days my wife went to Lima to talk things over with a representative of a foreign government to see if he could do anything. He replied: 'I believe I could do something at once to secure his liberty on condition that he goes directly on board ship and leaves the country.' My wife said to him: 'Mr. Consul, we have come to remain in Peru, and it has not entered our minds to leave it.'"

In his broken English Penzotti wrote to the Bible Society in New York: "To-day is sixteen days I am shut in the prison with the criminal people. The Catholic people are doing very much to make our work stop, but for all that I can see, they are lighting more the fire and doing the work good.

"In Peru the people are thinking of asking the government to grant them liberty of worship and the president is going to do all he can for it. Many distinguished people from the capital come to see me in my prison and want me to explain the Bible, and have much love for our work. The alcalde told me I am gaining more in these days of prison than in ten years of work. I am doing what I can with the prisoners. They have made a petition for me to preach to them Sundays."

It was in a dark, damp, underground dungeon that the priests had landed their quarry while they tried to prove that holding religious services for a handful of Protestants in a private room was illegal. This dungeon was an arched place built into the side of a hill, and had been used in the days of the Spaniards for a gun-powder vault. Now that it was occupied by human beings the people called it *Casas Matas,* or "The House that Kills." Penzotti found written on the wall of his cell a little Spanish verse. In English it is this:

> "Cell of my sorrows,
> Grave of living men;
> More terrible than death,
> Severer far than fetters."

The worst criminals in the State were kept here, any one of whom "would willingly have stuck a knife into him for $5 and a promise of freedom." Meals consisted entirely of raw peas and parboiled rice. The governor of the prison liked Penzotti and allowed him to receive visitors who often brought him food. Through them he continued to direct his work.

"My family and my congregation were also persecuted," he wrote. "However, they were not annihilated, but went on with the work without missing a single service during those months that I remained in prison."

The lawsuit dragged along as slowly as the priests could make it. Three times Penzotti was acquitted, and the case taken to a higher court. On the obsolete principle that a man is guilty until he can prove his innocence he was paying the penalty for what he had not done. Excitement over the case spread through the whole country. In Lima 2,000 people, among them the leading citizens of the city, held a mass meeting to agitate the question of religious liberty. The press and all liberal elements were roused in his favor, and when even political pressure had failed to free him, loud were the demands for a change in the constitution. So great was the popular interest in Penzotti's predicament that merchants referred to it in their business advertisements:

THE PENZOTTI QUESTION

RICE AND COCOA AT REASONABLE PRICES.

FOR SALE AT BLANK'S

On walls and sidewalks enthusiastic citizens expressed their sentiments in chalk. Some of these signs read: "Death to Penzotti! Down with all Protestants!" Others said: "Hurrah for Penzotti! Down with the priests!" Whenever the Penzotti children left the house they were followed by jeering mobs, and it became necessary to send the two oldest daughters to Santiago to school, so great was the danger and humiliation of their position in Callao.

Then help came from an unexpected quarter. A prominent New York mining engineer, Mr. E. E. Olcott, had been making a tour of the desolate mining regions of Peru. One Sunday morning just after he had returned to Lima from the wilderness, he saw a clipping from a New York paper saying that a Protestant missionary was confined in a Callao jail. He gave the item little thought, believing it to be merely newspaper talk. But after attending service at the little Episcopal church, he dropped in at the English Club to make inquiries from his acquaintances there.

"Any truth in that statement? Well, I should say so!" he was told. "You're a nice Christian to be going to church this morning! You ought to be doing something to get this man out of jail. Come down on the one o'clock train to Callao with me, and you'll have a chance to see for yourself."

That afternoon Mr. Olcott found Señor Penzotti out in the courtyard of the prison, surrounded by friends from his congregation. One woman who was there said to Mr. Olcott: "Oh, we must get him out from here. He is the first one who ever told me I could go directly to my Savior and talk things over. I always thought I had to go to the *padre*."

"Show me where you sleep," Mr. Olcott asked him. "They say that it's pretty hard." It was one large room, unlighted and unaired. At night the 165 prisoners, men and women, some of them murderers, were all huddled in there together to sleep as best they could on the damp floor.

"I'm going to send my photographer down here tomorrow," said Mr. Olcott when he was leaving. This was before the day of the kodak and snapshot.

"You can't get a picture without permission, and they will never give you permission," Penzotti told him.

It was two days before Mr. Olcott had to sail for New York. He went back to Lima and said to his young assistant: "I want you to go over to Callao to-morrow and take photographs of the cathedral and the post-office and the custom-house and the city hall. Then go down to the jail and find a prisoner there with a long, bushy black beard, named Penzotti. Get him to show you where he sleeps. When he goes inside, you stay outside and push the door shut. He'll look out of the window to see what's become of you. Then take a picture of him looking through the bars."

The next night the boy returned pale and trembling and so excited he could hardly tell what had happened. "They almost kept me in the jail too," he said. "I'd just taken the picture when a guard rushed down and wanted to know what I was doing. I told him I'd only just arrived, and I got away with the plates, but the police are after me!"

They set to work at once to develop the pictures. The plates were put to dry in an air bath and a little later Mr. Olcott came in with a lighted candle to see if they were behaving properly. A loud explosion followed. With his hair and eyebrows badly singed Mr. Olcott hastened to examine the oven, expecting to find his plates destroyed. But the explosion, it proved, had been in the lower part, and there on the top shelf sat the plates uninjured. The next day they were smuggled on board the steamer and hidden under the pillow in Mr. Olcott's stateroom.

The picture of Penzotti gazing from the prison window was published in the *New York Herald* with an article which caused extensive comment. Other influential people became interested, and diplomatic pressure was brought to bear. On the same day cablegrams from the Court of St. James and Washington reached Lima. "A taste of feudalism like this," said an editorial in the *Herald,* "gives us a new and strange sensation. When the Pope declares himself in favor of religious liberty it seems odd for one of the South American States, and that a Republic, to hang back. But we haven't any doubt that Peru will pull herself together and see that the stigma of imprisonment for religion's sake is wiped out."

"It is no longer Penzotti, a prisoner before the whole world," people said, "it is Peru which is a prisoner in the hands of the clergy."

Just three weeks after Mr. Olcott reached New York Penzotti was released from "The House that Kills." Years after the two men met in Panama when Penzotti embraced Mr. Olcott in true South American fashion and greeted him as *"Mi Salvador."*

"I left the prison at five o'clock in the afternoon, accompanied by a great number of people who surrounded and congratulated me. On the following Sunday the church was packed with people until there wasn't even room for a pin. From that time the work continued to grow without many persecutions or difficulties." The record of Bibles sold in Peru showed one result of the impetus which publicity gave the work: in 1892, 18,000 more were sold than in 1891.

After his acquittal Señor Penzotti called at the headquarters of the foreign legations in Lima. In a newspaper next day, one of the officials said this of him: "We were able to appreciate for ourselves the magnanimity which characterizes him. Not a single word of reproach fell from his lips, nor a single complaint against his persecutors."

He started at once on a trip down the coast to superintend the work of the Bible Society. That was Penzotti's way of taking a much-needed vacation.

The next year he was appointed agent for Central America and the Isthmus of Panama, and since 1908 he has superintended the work of the River Plate republics. His successor in Peru, Dr. Thomas B. Wood, wrote: "The work that Penzotti has accomplished in Peru as a founder and pioneer is a success that not many can gainsay. The way seems open to go up and possess the whole land." In November, 1915, the Roman Catholic clause of the constitution was struck out, and to-day any form of worship is legal.

"Now, on going to Peru," says Penzotti, "all doors are open to me except the prison doors, thanks to God."

W. BARBROOKE GRUBB

W. BARBROOKE GRUBB

W. BARBROOKE GRUBB

THE little Republic of Paraguay is cut in two by the River Paraguay. Along the eastern bank are rows of towns twinkling with electric lights at night time; across the river dark forests loom against the sky, and a lonely Indian camp-fire shines through the trees. On one side, the river steamers dock at busy wharves; on the other, gourds are rattling, and Indians chant weird songs. The civilized and the primitive are there side by side, with only the river between them.

The western section of Paraguay is a rank wilderness of swamps, thickets, and big trees, one of the most grewsome places in the world to travel about in. It is a part of *El Gran Chaco,* a desolate country of 200,000 square miles which extends down into northern Argentina. Horror and mystery still cling to the name Chaco—a name to conjure evil spirits with, the Paraguayans think. When expeditions used to appear there, bent on capturing slaves or subduing wild tribes, the natives would scurry out of the way like frightened animals; then slyly emerge from their hiding-places and murder their pursuers. Even the Jesuits, with their genius for putting a civilized finish on savages, never made any headway with the Chaco

Indians. A trip into their territory was once an adventure that few men lived to repeat, even though their errand was nothing more objectionable than surveying the land or collecting flower specimens.

The government once cared nothing for its Indian residents, and they had no share in the fortunes of the country. When Paraguay went to war they enjoyed it mightily. Said one old chief: "We heard firing and knew war was going on. We could not understand Christians killing each other—we only kill enemies; we never fight with members of our own tribe. We crossed over in our canoes at night to see what was the matter. We entered a house—no one there. We saw some cattle—no one in charge. We took all we could carry. The cattle we could not get to cross the river, so we killed all we could and took the meat. We continued to do this night after night. By day we feasted, by night we robbed. What a fine time we had! We wish the Christians would fight again."

In 1890 the South American Missionary Society—Allen Gardiner's Society—sent W. Barbrooke Grubb, then twenty-three years old, to explore and open up the country of the Lengua-Mascoy Indians, one of the two largest tribes living in the Paraguayan Chaco. The easiest thing for Grubb to do was to settle down near the river and civilization, and by making friends of the coast Indians gradually learn the customs and language of the tribe. Instead of this he decided to burn all his bridges behind him and strike right into the heart of the Chaco, where he could live among the people in their own wild, native haunts. No half-way measures appealed to Grubb. First he set out in a steam launch to see if the interior could be reached by water. He found that every stream was blocked by masses of reeds and rushes, and it was impossible for the little boat to nose her way through the tangle. Canoeing was particularly dangerous. For instance, "when attempting to land on a bank where an old alligator was sitting, it ran at the canoe open-mouthed, and our missionary planted his paddle in its mouth. This it crunched up like matchwood. He then gave it a piece of hard iron to chew, upon which it could make but little impression. While it firmly held the bar of iron in its mouth, Grubb jumped ashore and dispatched it with an ax."

So it was on foot and on horseback that Grubb pushed into the interior over the same wild trails where many a large party, heavily armed, had been assassinated by the Indians. People were horrified to learn that he had gone without guards or weapons, and with only a few unreliable river Indians for guides. "He hasn't a chance in a thousand," they said, and three times during his first expedition his death was reported. Once he had to paddle all night to reach a point where he could send word to the authorities that he was very much alive and not anxious to have an announcement of his murder sent home to his friends. He had already worked for four years among the savages of Tierra del Fuego, and the experience had taught him much. It was his policy to travel unprotected to show his friendliness and to prove that he had no fear; and he never admitted weakness by asking help from any chief, or by bribing the Indians with presents. To assume at all times and under all circumstances a dignified authority— that was Grubb's working plan.

On his first long trip he took five very reluctant Indian guides. Just as he arrived at an isolated village named Kilmesakthlapomap, "the place of burnt pigs," they refused to go on, fearful lest they be killed along with the foreigner. This left him stranded in a strange place, but instead of bargaining with them to stay he dismissed them curtly, and prepared to camp for the night. With a few words and many gestures he ordered one of the village Indians to water his horse, another to fill his kettle. "Beckoning to a woman," he says, "I pointed to a shady tree near by, and, sitting down upon the ground, gave her to understand that I would camp under that tree, and pointing to a fire I told her to take it and place it there for my convenience. I then walked around the village, beating off the dogs with my whip, and selected a piece of pumpkin here and a few potatoes there. These I gave to a man, and signed to him to put them under the tree where I intended to camp. By this time my horse had been brought back, so I unsaddled it, and then gave the lad instructions as well as I could to let it loose and to look after it." Finally he made up a bed on top of his baggage and went to sleep.

The Indians were so astonished at the fearlessness

of their visitor that they forgot to be suspicious. This must be a great white chief who knew perhaps even more wonderful things than their own wizards and witch-doctors. They decided to find out how easy it would be to take advantage of him. In the middle of the night two of them stole toward his camp, and began to extract bits of his property from the pile on which he was sleeping. All was breathlessly still. Then right in their ears sounded the biggest war-whoop Grubb knew how to make, and utterly terrified, they vanished in the darkness. The rest of the night he spent in peace.

Next morning Grubb sent for the chief of the village and told him he wanted guides, the salary to be a pair of cotton trousers for each man. The only Indian to volunteer was a witch-doctor who could not resist the temptation of owning a pair of white trousers with a British lion and "30 yds. Manchester" stamped in blue ink on one leg.

On returning to Villa Concepcion, his base of supplies, Grubb heard that the station of an English land company had been looted by a party of Indians. People laughed at him when he said he was going into the wilderness to catch the thieves and make them pay for all they had taken. He rode eighteen miles on the same horse with an old Indian who promised to show him the way. The culprits agreed to pay back in skins and feathers what they had stolen, on condition that he settle down and live with them. The presence of such a curiosity, they thought, would give them greater

prestige among other clans. Grubb cheerfully agreed
to the proposal, and set about establishing his first
settlement in the Chaco.

He directed his new friends to build him a hut of
palm-logs and sticks, with grass thatching, and to put
a bush in the doorway to keep out prowling dogs—a
necessary precaution, for it was considered bad luck
to kill a dog and each family owned at least three.
Provisions of sun-dried meat were hung from the
rafters, a tempting display to the Indian eye. One
night when he was snoozing on his sheepskin spread
out on the floor, Grubb heard some one stealthily tear-
ing a hole in the grass wall of his hut. From it
emerged a shaggy black head which he immediately
seized by the back hair. "I inquired who my visitor
was," he says, "and from muffled sounds I discovered
it was Alligator Stomach." This was a cook whose
chief failing was a fondness for sampling the soup
and meat, before he served it, until there was very
little left for any one else. "By way of explaining he
coolly told me that he had heard dogs near my hut, and
fearing for the safety of the meat he had simply come
to drive them out. Still retaining my hold of him, I
asked why he had gone to the trouble of breaking
through my wall instead of coming through the doorway, and told him that in my opinion he was the dog;
then, pushing his head roughly through the hole, I
bade him be gone."

Grubb had great sympathy with the native customs
of the Indians, and he wished to preserve all those not

directly harmful. The object of a missionary, as he puts it, "is to win men for Christ, and not to make them Englishmen." One foreign importation he refused to tolerate was the cheap whisky which coast Indians sometimes brought into the interior to sell. One day he was drinking a bitter dose of quinin mixture when an Indian came into his hut and caught sight of the medicine.

"Aha!" said the Indian, sniffing, "this smells like foreign liquor." And his expression seemed to add: "This stuff is bad for us, but I see *you* can drink it."

"If you will promise to say nothing about it, I will give you some of this," Grubb said to him.

His eyes gleaming with anticipation, the Indian gulped down a good dose; his face screwed up into lines of horror and surprise, and sputtering violently he vanished into the woods.

While on a hunting trip with the Indians, Grubb found a possible site for a mission station in a region called Thlagnasinkinmith, or "the place of many woodticks," and at once he began the process of moving. So far all provisions had been fetched from the river by Indian carriers, a laborious business not often to the taste of those selected to go.

One man, for instance, threatened to make serious trouble. It was too far and there would be too much to carry back, he said.

"Oh! What a mistake I have made!" exclaimed Grubb. "I thought I was speaking to one of the men, but I see it was one of the girls. Go away and weave blankets, my girl. Of course no one could expect you to go all the way to the river and carry heavy burdens."

All day long the Indian sulked. Then, armed and all ready to pick a quarrel, he came to Grubb and asked defiantly:

"Are you angry?"

"I am very angry!" said Grubb crisply and turned his back.

"I am just going to follow the men you have sent to the river, and help bring out your things," came a meek little voice behind him. There was no trifling with the great white chief!

Grubb determined to try the experiment of transporting supplies from the river to the new station by a cart and bullocks, and with the help of a few reluctant Indians, he cut the first track into the interior. The witch-doctors, who hated him because he laughed at their tricks, plotted to kill him by magic if he dared open up their wilderness to foreigners. But their threats added zest to the game. The trail was rough and in the rainy season almost impassable, but it has made history in the Chaco, for over it came the white men and civilization.

Two more missionaries were sent from England, and sixty miles further inland Grubb established a central station. When he came back to Thlagnasin-kinmith to move his property, he had to reprove the Indians for some fault, and as usual they took offense and deserted him.

For ten days he lived alone in his log hut. "The

wild scene around me," he wrote, "and the strange stillness so peculiar to the tropics, broken only by the weird sounds of insect and animal life, so worked upon my nerves that I imagined all the beasts of the forest were congregating nightly around my hut. The nearest human being, as far as I knew, was quite thirty miles off, and I had not even a dog as a companion." When a party of Indians finally appeared the only ones who would help with his bullock cart were two sulky old men and one boy. For seven long days, Grubb fought his way through marshes and forests and across rivers, almost single-handed, for one of the men was ill with fever, and the others usually stood by and watched when any hard work was to be done.

For five years Grubb lived the life of the Indians, roaming from village to village, first with one clan, then with another, learning their language and winning their confidence. He went hunting and camping with them, and when the day's game was unusually plentiful, he joined in their feasts and celebrations. "I used to enter heartily into these festivities, dancing and singing with them night after night, my face and arms painted red with *uruca* dye, my head adorned with feathers, and my body ornamented as far as possible in true Indian style." Like the rest he ate only once a day, and dipped his share of the repulsive food out of the greasy clay pot used in common by the whole company. The best water supply was found in the *caraguata* plant which holds about a pint in the hollow formed by its spiked leaves and thorns. This liquid the Indians would strain through the crown of a hat or a piece of old blanket to catch the water spiders and dead leaves. Often thirst drove them all to drink mud puddles or green, slimy water which even the animals refused to touch. One custom, whenever Indians met each other or sat around the camp-fire together, was to pass a common pipe from mouth to mouth. It was their way of being sociable, and it would have been a deadly insult to refuse the pipe or to wipe it off before smoking. Grubb's turn might come after an Indian who had been dining on a savoury rattlesnake, but he never flinched. He took part in wrestling matches and water sports, romped with the children, and chatted gayly with the women, whose favor was worth winning, for they held an important position in the community life. The men were all used to long marches from one hunting ground to another, and their powers of endurance, trained by years of continual wandering over the country, were tremendous. Grubb never allowed himself to betray his weariness. What they did, he did.

The deadly fear of evil spirits and the souls of departed friends prowling in the night casts a black shadow over the lives of the Chaco Indians until they have been taught to know better. No people in the world have a greater horror of ghosts, and nothing can make them venture away from their cluster of camps after the sun sets. After a death the burial rites are always performed before dark, and some-

times in such a hurry that a victim unfortunate enough
not to die earlier in the day is buried alive. Then, in
terror of the wandering spirit of the dead, the Indians
abandon and destroy the village where they have been
living and hurry on to build their wretched little
shelters somewhere else.

Grubb's influence became so great that, after much
reasoning with one clan on the occasion of an old
man's death, he made them promise not to destroy
their village as usual. But to be on the safe side they
pulled down all their huts and built more in a position
where they would be protected, by Grubb's own hut,
from the grave and the approaching ghost. Just a
few days before this the village witch-doctor had been
persuaded to build himself a real little cabin of which
he was very proud. This he could not bear to pull
down, so he blocked up the doorway and cut an opening on the opposite side—a device intended to baffle
the puzzled ghost, should he try to enter. The night
following the burial was a hideous one for all concerned.

"I was awakened by a terrible hubbub among the
people," says Grubb. "The few guns they had were
being fired off, arrows were whizzing through the air,
women were shrieking and beating on the ground with
sticks, children crying, dogs barking, and goats and
sheep running hither and thither." Some one had
dreamed that the ghost had entered Grubb's hut for a
little chat, and dreams were always believed. Any
communication with a departed spirit was considered

an unpardonable sin, and the angry people came to kill him. He offered to disprove their theory by walking over the grave; then, since that failed to satisfy them, he lay down on the floor again, drew the mosquito netting into place with a bored air, and apparently went to sleep. Perhaps the Indians were not anxious to have a second spirit ambling about the village, for they never carried out their threat. It was another mile-stone in the progress of Grubb's Chaco Mission. For the first time in their history, the Lengua-Mascoy Indians had remained in a village where death had occurred.

The witch-doctors were the greatest hindrance to establishing mission stations and their influence was always an evil one. Grubb never lost a chance to discredit them in the eyes of the people. Once a heavy rain did extensive damage to the village, and the wizard, supposed to have the power of raising storms whenever he liked, was the center of admiration. It so happened that his own garden was ruined by the rain. "Now," said Grubb to the crowd of Indians, "when he engineered that storm, why did he not arrange that it should not damage his own property?"

An hysterical old woman was supposed to be possessed of an evil spirit. While four men were holding her down and a wizard was trying to drive out the demon, Grubb strolled up with a bottle of strong liquid ammonia, and held it under the patient's nose. Her cure was instantaneous and complete. To find out how they managed their tricks, Grubb feigned a pain in his arm and sent for old Redhead, the witch-doctor. After sucking the painful spot, Redhead produced three fish-bones and announced that they had been wished upon him by some unfriendly wizard who lived in the western Chaco. "They are not nice people in the West," he said. "Quite different from us who love you and are your friends." Old Redhead's love was not apparent, however, when Grubb, taking him unawares, pried his mouth open and pulled out his whole secret store of fish-bones.

"We have to be very careful indeed," says Grubb of the Indians, "when appealing to their religious feelings, to avoid sensationalism, for they are easily worked upon, and the result would be a superficial rather than a permanent gain." In the whole Chaco Mission there is not a particle of the mysticism and glitter, none of the elaborate religious ceremonies which used to throw the Guarani Indians of the old Jesuit towns into emotional spasms which passed for religion. Simple exercises are sometimes held to honor men or women who have been plucky enough to lay aside a pet tradition. Four women, who had helped in the fight against infanticide by sparing the lives of four children each, were publicly praised, presented with printed certificates and crowned with flower wreaths, all on a raised platform where they could be shining examples of courage for the rest of the Indians.

Because the conversion of the Lengua-Mascoys is genuine and lasting when it does occur, the process

has been a long one. It was seven years before the
first church was built. In 1898 the first two converts
joined it—Philip and James they were called, because
their real names were too long to pronounce. In the
days of the Jesuits the priests commanded; the people
obeyed, and never learned how to depend on themselves. Grubb's policy is to guide his Indians till they
can direct their own lives along new lines, managing
their church, directing their schools and industries,
civilizing their own people. "I am perfectly sure of
one thing," says Mr. Grubb, "and that is, that until
the Indians themselves become the evangelists of their
own people we shall never succeed in building up a
powerful church." The very first convert was persuaded to give a little talk before his clan about the
things he had learned.

"These people," he said, pointing to Mr. Grubb and
the other missionaries of the station, "have told us that
a long time ago the Son of God came from above in
the form of a man, and lived in a country not very far
from their own. He preached his good news to the
people of that country, and they in turn told it to
others. This Son of God explains to us many things
we do not know, and shows us that our traditions are
wrong. We have known these people for some years,
and we have always found them truthful and friendly
to us. We are sure, therefore, that they are not deceiving us."

Repeatedly in the history of races primitive peoples
have gradually dwindled and disappeared after com-

ing in contact with civilization, which has far too often meant customs, clothing, and manners most appropriate for white men but ridiculously unsuitable for savages. Mr. Grubb's is the magnificent creed of modern missions: "To arrest the decline and decay of the race; to bind the various tribes together; to give them a system of government; to raise them to the level of property-holders; to induce them to adopt an industrious, settled, and regular life; to instil into them a higher moral sense; to awaken a desire for culture and progress; to fit them to receive the offer of the Paraguayan government of citizenship in that Republic; to make them useful members of society, a people who could bear their part in the development of their own land, and take their due place as a unit in the growing population of a great continent. The only way we could succeed in doing this was by implanting in them a pure, living form of Christianity, which would become the basis of their political, social, and moral constitution."

To-day in the heart of the Chaco there is a village called the Garden Colony of Enmakthlawaia where each Indian owns his own house, garden, and cattle, earns his living by a good trade, has money put away in the Indian bank, knows how to read and write, and sends his children to school. The men of this village make their own laws and see that they are enforced. When they decree that no witch-craft can be practised within the village boundaries, and along comes a party of outsiders to indulge in wizards' tricks, native policemen sally forth and use their "billies" to good advantage.

The day is passed when tourists dare not enter the Chaco. "Before I arrived in South America," says one Englishman who visited the Garden Colony in idle curiosity, "I knew no one connected with the mission, and, having nothing to do with missionary work, my criticism is absolutely that of an outsider. They really do seem to be building up and educating the Indian on such excellent lines that I firmly believe it will prove of a permanent character, and eventually become a self-governing body. When one thinks that but ten years ago it was dangerous to one's life to venture into the Chaco, while now there are numerous *estancias* on the border, and one can now go for a hundred and more miles into the interior with comparative safety, it shows that the missionaries have got the 'thin edge of the wedge' well thrust in.

"These men and women are making savages into reasonable, peace-abiding people, and—what touches the commercial world more—they are making what was once considered a piece of waste land, the size of England and Scotland, of real commercial value. Landowners in the Paraguayan Chaco owe all this to the English Mission, and especially to Mr. W. B. Grubb, the pioneer and backbone of the whole undertaking."

The story of the Chaco Mission, like that of all great achievements, leaves untold half the adventures and dangers and difficulties that are calmly accepted

as all a part of the day's program. They are the
privilege of explorers, scientists, sea-captains, bridge-
builders, missionaries—all the men who lead the way
for others to follow. A tourist in Paraguay said of
the Chaco missionaries: "Like the plucky young fellows they are, they seem to have concealed the real
hardships they endure."

But Mr. Grubb, when he looks backward, will tell
you that those early years, exploring the wilderness
and living as the Indians lived, were the happiest in
his whole life.

BIBLIOGRAPHY

FRANCISCO PIZARRO

Andagoya, Pascual de. *Narrative of the Proceedings of Pedrarias Davila.* 1865. Translated by C. R. Markham. Hakluyt Society, London. Out of print.

Bryce, James. *South America: Observations and Impressions.* 1914. (Revised edition.) The Macmillan Company, New York. $2.50.

Cieza de Léon, Pedro de. *The War of Quito: Inca Documents.* 1913. Translated by C. R. Markham. Hakluyt Society, London. Out of print.

Fiske, John. *The Discovery of America.* 2 Vols. 1892. Houghton, Mifflin & Company, New York. $1.80 each.

Guzman, Alonzo Enrique de. *Life and Acts, 1518-43.* 1862. Translated by C. R. Markham. Hakluyt Society, London. Out of print.

Helps, Arthur. *The Spanish Conquest in America.* 4 Vols. 1904. John Lane, New York. $1.50 each. Book XVII, "The Conquest of Peru."

Markham, Clements R. *History of Peru.* 1892. Charles H. Sergel & Company, Chicago, $2.50.

Prescott, William. *History of the Conquest of Peru.* 2 Vols. 1847. T. Y. Crowell & Company, New York. $1.25.

Robertson, William. *The History of America.* 2 Vols. 1778. W. Strahan, London. Reprinted, Library of American History, Samuel L. Knapp. Vol. II, Book VI.

Vega, Garcilasso de la. *Royal Commentaries of the Incas.* Vol. II. 1871. Translated by C. R. Markham. Hakluyt Society, London. Out of print.

Xerez, Francisco de. (Pizarro's secretary.) *Reports on the Discovery of Peru.* 1872. Translated by C. R. Markham. Hakluyt Society, London. Out of print.

JOSÉ DE ANCHIETA

Dawson, Thomas C. *South American Republics.* 2 Vols. 1904. G. P. Putnam's Sons, New York. $3.00.

Graham, R. B. Cunninghame. *A Vanished Arcadia.* 1901. The Macmillan Company, New York. $2.50.

Koebel, W. H. *In Jesuit Land.* 1912. Stanley Paul & Company, London. 12s. 6d.

Southey, R. *History of Brazil.* 3 Vols. 1817-22. Longman, Hurst, Rees, Orme & Brown, London. Out of print.

Zahm, J. A. Rev. *Through South America's Southland.* 1916. D. Appleton & Company, New York. $2.50, net.

Brazilian Biographical Manual. "Anchieta, José de."

Catholic Encyclopedia. "Anchieta, José de."

JOSÉ DE SAN MARTIN

Crichfield, George W. *American Supremacy.* 2 Vols. Vol. I. 1908. Brentano's, New York. $6.00, net.

Dawson, Thomas C. *South American Republics.* 2 Vols. 1904. G. P. Putnam's Sons, New York. $3.00.

Elliott, G. F. Scott. *Chile: Its History and Development.* 1907. Charles Scribner's Sons, New York. $3.00.

Hall, Captain Basil. *Extracts from a Journal Written on the Coasts of Chile, Peru, and Mexico, 1820, 1821, 1822.* 2 Vols. 1824. Archibald Constable & Company, Edinburgh. Vol. I.

Mitre, Bartolomé. *The Emancipation of South America.* (Condensed translation of the History of San Martin, Buenos Aires, 1887.) 1893. Translated by William Pilling. Chapman & Hall, London. 12s. Out of print.

Edinburgh Review, Vol. XIII : 277. January, 1809. "The Emancipation of Spanish America," a review.

SIMON BOLIVAR

Bingham, Hiram. *The Journal of an Expedition Across Venezuela and Colombia, 1906, 1907.* 1909. Yale University Press, New Haven. $2.25.

Cochrane, Charles Stuart. *Journal of a Residence and Travels in Colombia during the Years 1823 and 1824.* 1825. H. Colburn, London. $7.50.

Crichfield, George W. *American Supremacy.* 2 Vols. 1908. Brentano's, New York. $6.00, net.

Dawson, Thomas C. *South American Republics.* 2 vols. 1904. G. P. Putnam's Sons, New York. $3.00.

Mitre, Bartolomé. *The Emancipation of South America.* (Condensed translation of the History of San Martin, Buenos Aires, 1887.) 1893. Translated by William Pilling. Chapman & Hall, London. 12s. Out of print.

Petre, F. Loraine. *Simon Bolivar;* "El Libertador." 1910. John Lane, New York. $4.00.

Recollections of a Service of Three Years in Venezuela and Colombia. By an Officer of the Colombian Navy. 1828. 2 Vols. Hunt & Clarke, London.

JAMES THOMSON

Brown, Hubert W. *Latin America.* 1901. Fleming H. Revell Company, New York. $1.20, net.

Browning, Webster E. "The Lancasterian Schools in South America." Report of Commission III, Congress on Christian Work in Latin America. 1916. Missionary Education Movement, New York. 3 Vols. $2.50.

Thomson, James. *Letters on the Moral and Religious State of South America.* Written during a residence of nearly seven years in Buenos Aires, Chile, Peru, and Colombia. 1827. James Nisbet, London.

ALLEN F. GARDINER

Gardiner, Allen F. *A Visit to the Indians on the Frontiers of Chile.* 1841. R. B. Seelye and W. Burnside, London.

Hirst, W. A. *Argentina.* 1912. Charles Scribner's Sons, New York. $3.00.

Maitland, Francis J. G. *Chile: Its Land and People.* 1914. Francis Griffiths, London. 10s. 6d.

Marsh, John W., and Stirling, W. H. *The Story of Allen Gardiner.* 1874. James Nisbet & Company, London. 1s. 6d.

Myers, Sarah A. *Self-Sacrifice, or The Pioneers of Fuegia.* 1861. Westminster Press, Philadelphia. Out of print.

Snow, William Parker. *A Two Years' Cruise off Tierra del Fuego.* 1857. (Late Commander of the Mission Yacht *Allen Gardiner*.) Longman, Brown, Green, Longmans & Roberts, London. 2 Vols.

Williams, Richard. *Journal of a Mission, 1850, 1851, a Contemporary Transcript.* (In manuscript only).

Young, Robert. *From Cape Horn to Panama.* 1900. South American Missionary Society, London. 2s. 6d.

Harper's Magazine, Vol. XI: 607. October, 1855. "The Araucanians," a review.

The Living Age, Vol. XXXIII: 544. June 19, 1852. "Starvation of Patagonian Missionaries."

JUAN MANUEL ROSAS

Crichfield, George. *American Supremacy.* 2 Vols. 1908. Brentano's, New York. $6.00, net.

Dawson, Thomas C. *South American Republics.* 2 Vols. 1904. G. P. Putnam's Sons, New York. $3.00.

Hirst, W. A. *Argentina.* 1912. Charles Scribner's Sons, New York. $3.00.

Parish, Sir Woodbine. *Buenos Aires and the Provinces of the Rio de la Plata.* 1839. J. Murray, London.

Sarmiento, D. F. *The Days of the Tyrants; or Civilization and Barbarism;* with a biographical sketch of the author by Mrs. Horace Mann. 1868. Thomas Nelson & Sons, New York.

Cornhill Magazine, Vol. V: 530, New Series. October, 1898. "Rosas."

Democratic Review, Vol. XVIII: 369. May, 1846. "Rosas—Struggle of the Republican against the Monarchical Principle in the Argentine Republic."

Eclectic Magazine, Vol. XXVI: 352, "Don Manuel Rosas"; and 406, "Rosas and La Plata." July, 1852.

Fraser, Vol. XLV: 596. May, 1852. "Rosas, the Dictator of Buenos Aires."

North American Review, Vol. LXIX: 43. July, 1849. "Rosas and the Argentine Republic," a review.

Overland Monthly, Vol. I: 337. October, 1868. "The Story of a Dictator."

DOMINGO F. SARMIENTO

Akers, Charles E. *A History of South America.* 1912. E. P. Dutton, New York. $4.00.

Crichfield, George W. *American Supremacy.* 2 Vols. 1908. Brentano's, New York. $6.00, net.

Sarmiento, D. F. *The Days of the Tyrants; or Civilization and Barbarism;* with a biographical sketch of the author by Mrs. Horace Mann. 1868. Thomas Nelson & Sons, New York.

DOM PEDRO II

Agassiz, J. Louis, and Mrs. Elizabeth Cabot. *A Journey in Brazil.* 1871. Houghton, Mifflin & Company, New York. $2.50.

Andrews, C. C. *Brazil: Its Condition and Prospects.* 1889. D. Appleton & Company, New York. $1.50.

Bruce, G. J. *Brazil and the Brazilians.* 1914. Dodd, Mead & Company, New York. $3.00, net.

Dawson, Thomas C. *South American Republics.* 2 Vols. 1904. G. P. Putnam's Sons, New York. $3.00.

Kidder, D. P., and Fletcher, J. C. *Brazil and the Brazilians.* 1857. Childs & Peterson, Philadelphia. Out of print.

Vincent, Frank. *Around and About South America.* 1890. D. Appleton & Company, New York. $5.00.

The Arena, Vol. V: 366. February, 1892. "The Last American Monarch."

The Contemporary Review, Vol. LXXXVI: 727. November, 1904. "The Last Emperor of Brazil."

The Cosmopolitan, Vol. VIII: 431. February, 1890. "The Exiled Emperor."

The Nation, Vol. XLIX: 494. December 19, 1889. "The Brazilian Revolution."

F   40   G

North American, Vol. LXVIII: 314. April, 1849. "The Empire of Brazil," a review.
Smithsonian Institution Report, 1876, p. 173. "Dom Pedro II, Emperor of Brazil."

DAVID TRUMBULL

Speer, Robert E. *Studies of Missionary Leadership.* 1914. Westminster Press, Philadelphia. $1.50.
Trumbull, Henry Clay. *Old Time Student Volunteers.* 1902. Fleming H. Revell Company, New York. $1.00.
New Englander and Yale Review, Vol. XIV: 430, New Series. June, 1889. "In Memoriam: Rev. David Trumbull, D.D., Valparaiso, Chile."
The Record (Valparaiso), February 23, 1889. "In Memoriam."
Annual Reports of the Presbyterian Board of Foreign Missions.

FRANCISCO PENZOTTI

Laun, Rev. Friedrich. *The Chief Points of Difference between the Catholic and Protestant Creeds.* 1915. (Roman Catholic.) J. F. Wagner, New York. 75 cents, net.
Penzotti, F. *Spiritual Victories in Latin America.* Autobiography. 1916. Translated by Miss Bertha Bell. American Bible Society, New York. 5 cents.
Annual Reports of American Bible Society, 1883-1894.
The Bible Society Record, 1884-1891.
The New York Herald, January 13, 20, 26; March 9, 1892.

W. BARBROOKE GRUBB

Grubb, W. B. *Among the Indians of the Paraguayan Chaco.* 1904. South American Missionary Society, London. 1s. 6d.
Grubb, W. B. *An Unknown People in an Unknown Land.* 1911. J. B. Lippincott Company, Philadelphia. $3.50.
Grubb, W. B. *A Church in the Wilds.* 1914. E. P. Dutton & Company, New York. $1.50, net.